The Poster Art of A. M. CASSANDRE

The Poster Art of
A.M.CASSANDRE

ROBERT K. BROWN & SUSAN REINHOLD
E. P. DUTTON · New York

Frontispiece: Original gouache study for an unpublished poster created for Dubonnet. 1932. 63⅛" x 47½" (160.3 x 120.6 cm). Collection Barry Friedman, Ltd., New York.

First published, 1979,
in the United States by E.P. Dutton, New York.

All rights reserved under
International and Pan-American Copyright Conventions.

No part of this publication may
be reproduced or transmitted in any form
or by any means, electronic or mechanical, including
photocopy, recording or any information storage
and retrieval system now known or to be invented,
without permission in writing from the publisher,
except by a reviewer who wishes to quote brief passages
in connection with a review written for inclusion
in a magazine, newspaper or broadcast.

For information contact:
E.P. Dutton, 2 Park Avenue, New York, N.Y. 10016

Library of Congress Catalog Card Number: 79-51142

Printed and bound by
South China Printing Co., Limited, Hong Kong.

ISBN: 0-525-18175-X (cloth)
ISBN: 0-525-47602-4 (DP)

Published simultaneously in Canada by
Clarke, Irwin & Company Limited, Toronto and Vancouver

Design: Dorothy Schmiderer

10 9 8 7 6 5 4 3 2 1

First Edition

CONTENTS

ACKNOWLEDGMENTS vi

INTRODUCTION 1

I. A. M. Cassandre in the Development of Poster Art 1

II. The Life of A. M. Cassandre 3

III. Cassandre's Style 12

IV. Posterography: 1922–1939 19

NOTES 22

SELECTED BIBLIOGRAPHY 23

INDEX TO THE COLOR PLATES 89

ACKNOWLEDGMENTS

As is often the case with applied artists, a dearth of published information about their lives is nearly always the rule. Therefore we are exceedingly grateful to several people who shared with us their oral histories of A. M. Cassandre. Above all we are indebted to Henri Mouron, Cassandre's son, who provided us with unique information about his father's life. We are also grateful to two artists, André François and Raymond Mason, who shared their reminiscences of and experiences with Cassandre. Some published material we might have overlooked was graciously provided by Madame Sylvie Lorant, who is writing her doctoral dissertation on Cassandre at the Sorbonne, and the graphic designer Leo Rackow.

We should also like to thank three art historians who were most helpful in leading us to sources that we could study for the section on Cassandre's pictorial style. Robert Rosenblum of the New York University Institute of Fine Art brought our attention to Christopher Green's penetrating book, *Léger and the Avant-Garde*. Christopher Green himself took time out of his busy schedule at the Courtauld Institute of Art in London to give us his impressions of Cassandre's work. However, the greatest debt of gratitude is reserved for Jonathan M. Brown, also of the New York University Institute of Fine Art, who not only pointed out several illuminating aspects of Cassandre's work, but was responsible ten years ago for making his brother Robert aware of Cassandre's posters.

We also wish to thank Bill Hayward of New York who took valuable time away from his less mundane assignments to photograph most of the posters that appear in this book.

Finally, we wish to acknowledge all of the collectors and dealers who generously made available for reproduction their Cassandre posters, as well as the individuals at several museums who allowed us to look through their holdings and select the posters we required for this book:

David Bergman and Robert Helsley; Mr. and Mrs. David Bradford; Linda diLiberto; Mr. and Mrs. Richard F. Feiner; Barry Friedman, Ltd., New York; Frank Fristachi; Stephan Ganeles, New York; Mr. and Mrs. Herbert Goldman; Frank Latorre; Herbert Matter; Susan J. Pack; Mr. and Mrs. Peter Rauch; Ada Strove, Curator of Applied Art, Stedelijk Museum, Amsterdam; Richard Took and Ronne Baer, Rights and Reproductions Department, The Museum of Modern Art, New York; Alain Weill, Curator of The Poster Archive, Musée des Arts Décoratifs, Paris; and Karl Wobmann, Curator of The Poster Collection, Kunstgewerbemuseum der Stadt Zürich.

New York, 1979

SUSAN REINHOLD
ROBERT K. BROWN

INTRODUCTION

I. A. M. Cassandre in the Development of Poster Art

In the relatively brief history of commercial poster art—one that virtually parallels in the number of years the history of modern art itself—only a small group of poster artists can unequivocally be considered as masters whose contributions exceeded their lifetimes and provided connecting links to the forward development of the medium. This group would certainly comprise Jules Chéret, Henri de Toulouse-Lautrec, the Beggarstaffs (James Pryde and William Nicholson), Lucian Bernhard, and A. M. Cassandre.

It was Chéret who harnessed the capabilities of color lithography in 1869 [1] and used them to create gay, eye-catching, and decorative images with harmonious lettering that convinced the businessmen of the day that posters could indeed be an effective means of advertising. Toulouse-Lautrec, by virtue of the more than thirty posters he designed between 1891 and 1900, was significant in two respects: first, that a fine painter and printmaker could express himself without compromise in making posters and second, by emphasizing the plastic elements of draftsmanship in a clear, uncluttered fashion while eliminating the need for information and its attendant emphasis on large, unharmonious, and extraneous lettering.

In the handful of posters executed by the Beggarstaffs during the one-year period between 1894 and 1895,[2] the effectiveness of a minimalist approach—as shown by their use of untouched and expansive areas around and among the simply executed subject matter of their posters and their refusal to fill up pictorial space with anything beyond absolutely basic and essential text—served as an effective antidote to the typical posters of the period.

As a poster designer who was directly influenced by Toulouse-Lautrec and the Beggarstaffs, the German interior designer, typographer, and poster artist Lucian Bernhard refined their aesthetic by making posters as early as 1903 that reduced graphic design to its most basic elements in new and bold ways. In such works as *Priester Matches, Stiller Shoe,* and a poster for Manoli depicting an open box with one of its cigarettes propped against its side, only the product and its name against a solid-colored background comprise the entire design. Although Bernhard himself admitted that he had limitations as a draftsman [3] (a shortcoming that he used to good advantage in simplifying his designs), he was a master typographer who was so adept that he was able to model his letters with much the same form that he gave to many of his images.

If there is one common and compelling contribution that these poster artists made to commercial poster design, it is that they took it from the primitive and naïve notion that advertising posters had to be filled with complex detail and a plethora of information to approaches that became exercises in solving problems of design. Furthermore, as the years progressed and as each of these poster artists came into prominence, their works became less like illustrative art and more characteristic of something that evolved into a unique and truly distinctive medium.

By 1923, the year when A. M. Cassandre made the first poster he considered to be truly his own—*Au Bûcheron*—the development of poster art since World War I was no longer influenced primarily by commercial artists, but also by modern architects and, even

A. M. Cassandre, as photographed by Herbert Matter, in Central Park, New York, in 1939. Photograph courtesy Herbert Matter.

more so, by avant-garde painters. The painters, especially, began to use posters with increasing frequency to announce cultural events and in so doing, left examples in poster form of the various experimental art movements of the early twentieth century, such as German Expressionism, Russian Constructivism, Dada, and the Bauhaus, among others. These "cultural" posters were printed in small quantities and directed at elitist audiences without concession to commercialism and popular taste. It certainly can be said that this type of poster influenced the young Cassandre and that he filled much of the gap between the avant-garde cultural poster and the commercial poster.

Although this was one of Cassandre's great contributions to the history and development of poster art, he was even more inspired by the paintings of the avant-garde than by its posters. Had circumstances been such that Cassandre lived in another place and time than Paris in the late 1910s and early 1920s, it is questionable that any greatness he might have achieved would have been as a poster designer, so inspired was he by the artistic climate around him. Given his way of seeing the real world and the world of art, any posters he might have done otherwise would certainly have been much different.

Although the details of Cassandre's everyday life during his formative years as poster designer are no longer known, it is clear that he must have spent a great deal of time looking at the advanced art of the day and immersing himself in the life of the city and its new design and technology. It is a near-certainty, according to his son, Henri Mouron, that he visited the aviation and automobile salons, for he enjoyed a lifelong fascination with automobiles, going so far as to marry the daughter of one of France's biggest car manufacturers. He was also a friend and admirer of Le Corbusier and asked him in the mid-1920s to design a villa in Versailles, the plans of which he ultimately rejected before settling on those of another famous modern architect, Auguste Perret. His most revealing friendship, however, was with the poet Blaise Cendrars. Besides having in common with Cassandre the experience of growing up in Russia,[4] Cendrars had social and working relationships that probably cut the widest swath of anyone's through the Parisian avant-garde. Cendrars's dynamic, vibrant, and powerful enthusiasm for contemporary big-city life—and everything that was new in it—exerted in his poetry and other artistic endeavors a profound influence on the poetry, painting, and music of the 1910s and 1920s, as he worked and fraternized with such diverse individuals as Robert Delaunay, Guillaume Apollinaire, Fernand Léger, Abel Gance, Erik Satie, and Darius Milhaud, among others.[5]

To conclude that Cassandre's posters were in step with the Parisian avant-garde of the 1920s would not be correct. By the time Cassandre made his first great posters in the early and mid-1920s, Braque, Picasso, and Gris had abandoned their synthetic Cubism for a more curvilinear Cubist style, and the "biomorphic" paintings of Arp and Miró, as well as the beginning of Surrealism, comprised the leading edge of contemporary or avant-garde painting. Nevertheless, Cassandre was a keen observer of modern trends in art and was able to store and call upon them —sometimes years after the fact—when he felt that certain ideas and techniques would contribute to his purpose and at the same time appeal to the general public whose consciousness and receptivity lagged behind those of the innovators in art.

In spite of Cassandre's keen interest in modern art and the influences it had on his posters, he believed that painting and postermaking were two separate activities. In one of his most-quoted sayings, he postulated that, "The poster is only a means to an end, a means of communication between the dealer and the public, something like telegraphy. The poster plays the part of a telegraph official: he does not initiate news, he merely dispenses it. No-one asks him for his opinion. He is only required to bring about a clear, good and exact connection."[6] When Cassandre conceived of spaces upon which to create his images, he did not think of them as canvases but as the streets of the city. He was very much aware that almost everybody, as they hurried about their business, would not stop to look at or to contemplate a poster that was involuntarily placed before them. So, in spite of the changes in pictorial style he often went through, the one aspect common to the majority of Cassandre's posters was an uncluttered and simple directness that, on the one hand, could be consumed "en passant," but on the other, contained subtleties that gave the posters their greatness and that could be isolated by those who took the time to study them. In his own words Cassandre summed up the relationship between the man in the street and the posters he encountered: "Today's man is in a hurry, in a hurry to get where? One wonders about it, but it is a fact that he is hurried, hurried, and impatient. He hasn't the time to split hairs. He admires brevity, concision, the straight line, prefers violence over force, the cry to conversation, and Château Yquem cocktails. That is why he loves the poster and why for him it is his most authentic expression."[7]

As steeped as Cassandre was in avant-garde painting, he was not the first commercial poster artist that was influenced by such painters as Léger, Delaunay, and the Italian Futurists, although, as we shall see, he was much more forceful and dynamic than any other in showing their influences. However, one designer who was both a predecessor and a contemporary of Cassandre (and of whom Cassandre was certainly aware) showed occasional flashes of how posters adapted tendencies of the avant-garde. The artist was the American-born Edward McKnight Kauffer, who did his greatest posters in England. Two posters by him that are dated 1922 are particularly noteworthy. In *London History at the London Museum,* which depicts the Fire of London, Kauffer creates a rather Expressionistic stage-set effect of flames and black and white smoke that dwarfs three silhouetted small buildings. The solid orange, yellow, and brown columns of smoke are juxtaposed one against the other in a manner suggesting Delaunay's simultanist paintings, while their tall, gracefully curved abstracted shapes are reminiscent of the forms of Natalia Gontcharova was concerned with in her painting at the time.

Kauffer also did a few posters advertising department store winter sales for London Transport. The most impressive and dramatic was one showing colored silhouettes of women shoppers being blown around in a mottled, swirling disk of blue, white, and gray that not only draws again on the simultaneity of Delaunay but also on the movement and interaction with the environment, a major characteristic of Italian Futurism and the related English Vorticist movement, which Kauffer knew firsthand after his arrival in London around the beginning of World War I.

With these and other posters before 1925, Kauffer almost made the sort of breakthroughs that Cassandre was to achieve. What held Kauffer back from developing a consistent, truly dramatic and dynamic style earlier on was a strong influence on his work by the prewar German postermakers, notably Lucian Bernhard and Ludwig Hohlwein, and the lack of opportunity to deal often with modern subjects and the new technology resulting from the more romantic and less dynamic concerns of London and British society.

Other poster artists also flirted with ideas of the avant-garde painters and graphic designers. Several experimented with the notions of figurative mass that came out of Cézanne and the Cubists. At other times, the subject matter of posters would be conducive to a modernistic approach and would lead their designers to use hefty modeling and Italian Futurist force lines to connote speed and movement in automobile and aviation posters. Yet, as with Kauffer, the difference between them and Cassandre was they also were tentative in breaking away from what had become an established style, developed primarily from the German designers and Cappiello and his followers, to the conscious aim of Cassandre, which was to conceive successfully an overtly dynamic, geometric, and powerful postermaking style.

II.   The Life of A. M. Cassandre

A. M. Cassandre was born Adolphe Jean-Marie Mouron on January 24, 1901,[8] in the Ukrainian city of Kharkov. His father was one of four sons raised in Bordeaux. As was common in many bourgeois families, the sons had no choice of a profession because of financial considerations. In order to seek his freedom, Cassandre's father ran away to Russia at age seventeen to join his uncle, who imported French wine. It was a prosperous business, and when the uncle died, Cassandre's father inherited it. Although the father married a Russian, he despised Russians in general and sent his children to France for their schooling each year. Cassandre, who was the youngest, eventually had to remain in France permanently because of the outbreak of World War I, and his family shortly thereafter had to leave Russia because of the Revolution, leaving the business and their possessions to the Bolsheviks. Although the family was ruined, the father supported Cassandre in his wish to become an artist, recognizing that he himself had refused to be forced into a livelihood he did not desire.

When Cassandre was seventeen, he entered the École des Beaux-Arts, which he walked out on after one hour.[9] Next he studied with a minor painter named Lucien Simon at the Académie Julien, where he made paintings in the style of Cézanne—a significant fact as Cézanne also influenced many of the artists who were to influence Cassandre. Although none of Cassandre's student work exists, it was, according to his son, less concerned with color than with composition, again an important approach that became evident in his poster design.

In order to earn money for his art studies and living expenses, Cassandre took a job with the printing firm of Hachard et Compagnie on Place Madeleine. Although he at first did rather routine work there, by 1922 he began making posters that he signed "A. M. Cassandre," a pseudonym he took for no apparent reason other than the connotation it has of foretelling dire events to which no one pays attention. Because Cassandre considered *Au Bûcheron* (1923) as his first original poster, one can assume that the posters that preceded it, *Sadac* and *À Moi les Vraies Pâtes Garres,* were made under someone else's direction.

In 1923, Cassandre met Madeleine Richard, the daughter of Max Richard and niece of Georges Richard, the largest automobile manufacturers in France at the time. When they were married in 1924,

it marked the third marriage for his wife, with the previous two having produced four children. A year later, Cassandre's only child, Henri Mouron, was born. The marriage ended in divorce in 1939. Cassandre was remarried, around 1944, to Nadine Robinson, who made dresses and theatre costumes.

From 1923 until 1928, Cassandre continued making posters for Hachard. Despite the several masterpieces he turned out for the firm—the first *Au Bûcheron, PiVolo, L'Intransigeant, Étoile du Nord,* and *Nord Express*—there were many posters he did that paled by comparison. In general they suffered from inelegant, blocky lettering and heavy and conflicting geometric forms. Cassandre realized this when he selected the posters for the monograph on himself that was published in 1948 by the Swiss publisher Zollikofer et Compagnie. But by 1927, Cassandre's career and talents hit full stride. He was receiving prize commissions, the most prestigious of which were from the French National Railways. He also found himself in demand by the Dutch and English, for whom he produced some of his best designs.

In 1929 Cassandre made his first foray into commercial typography. He had met the well-known type founder Charles Peignot at the 1925 Exposition des Arts Décoratifs,[10] and when they finally collaborated four years later, it was on a new type face named Bifur. Although Peignot used and publicized it often in his celebrated magazine *Arts et Métiers Graphiques,* the upper-case bifurcated display type never quite caught on. The same result was to happen the following year when Cassandre gave Peignot another new display type called L'Acier.

Cassandre's third marketed type design, which, after several years of research and experimentation, resulted in the Peignot, proved to be a success as well as a major contribution to modern typography. As the Deberny & Peignot catalogue of 1936 described it, "Cassandre has decided to abandon the cursive handwritten, lower-case forms which the printing trade inherited from the fifteenth-century humanists. These forms themselves were copies of the ninth-century letter shapes which were, in fact, nothing more than an embellished form of the scribbled Merovingian distortions of inscriptional capitals."[11]

(*Opposite*). *Droste's Verpleegster Cacao.* c.1929. Publisher not given. 23″ x 16½″ (58.5 x 42 cm). Collection Stedelijk Museum, Amsterdam.

(*Above right*). Bifur alphabet. 1929. From *Paris 1929* (Paris: Charles Moreau, 1929), plate 65. Collection Mark Weinbaum, New York.

(*Right*). Peignot alphabet, upper and lower cases. 1936. Courtesy Bruce Barton.

In designing the Peignot, Cassandre created two alphabets; an upper case and a lower case, the latter actually comprised of small capitals with lower-case characteristics. Although the lower-case Peignot seems more graceful, modern, and innovative, owing in large measure to the use of ascenders and descenders and the combining of pure capital and calligraphic forms,[12] the upper case has been the much more widely used, even though one now sees increased use of the lower case. Nonetheless, despite its resurgence, the Peignot has remained a display type used in posters, packaging, brochures, and television graphics, as opposed to books, magazines, and newspapers for which it was also intended.

In his later years Cassandre designed several typefaces for Olivetti typewriters and, as his last self-absorbing creative endeavor, he designed a typeface he named La Métope, the word used for the square area between a certain kind of ornament called a triglyph found in Doric friezes. Because La Métope was considered unorthodox—its imaginary horizontal plane went through the letters instead of being at the bottom—it was rejected by a German publisher whose discouraging letter was found on Cassandre's desk when his suicide was discovered on June 17, 1968.

To return to 1930, Cassandre founded Alliance Graphique with another well-known poster designer, Charles Loupot, and a twenty-six-year-old printers' representative from the north, Maurice Moyrand. Moyrand's family knew the owners of the L. Danel printing firm in Lille, which had published several of Cassandre's posters for the French National Railways between 1928 and 1932. Cassandre had met Moyrand in 1926,[13] and it was through this relationship that Moyrand was able to bring Cassandre and the L. Danel firm together. More a serious design studio than an advertising agency because of Cassandre's and Loupot's talents and the high artistic standards of Moyrand, Alliance Graphique prospered. Many of the best posters in France came out of the studio in the Eighteenth Arrondissement, including several by another illustrious French poster artist, Jean Carlu. On September 15, 1934, Moyrand was killed in an automobile accident, and without his leadership, Alliance Graphique was closed down the following year.[14]

In addition to his various design activities during the late 1920s and the early 1930s—ones that also included creating brochures and catalogues for such firms as Nicolas and Dubonnet—Cassandre briefly tried his hand at running a small school of art and graphic design. In 1934 and 1935, he had the school on rue Ferou, not far from Place St.-Sulpice. (Prior to this, Cassandre also did some teaching at the École des

(*Opposite above*). Advertising specimen for Alliance Graphique, Paris, 1932. 11⅝″ x 8⅞″ (29.7 x 22.4 cm). Collection Reinhold-Brown Gallery, New York.

(*Opposite below*). Cover for *Nord Magazine*, 3, no. 5, May 1930. Collection Leo Rackow.

(*Above left*). Cover for Nicolas wine catalogue for 1936. Designed 1935. Draeger Frères, Paris. Collection Reinhold-Brown Gallery, New York.

(*Above right*). Original watercolor design for a Nicolas wine brochure. 1930. 9″ x 7″ (22.8 x 17.8 cm). Collection David Bergman and Robert Helsley.

(*Left*). *Tabac Kisroul*. 1935. Säuberlin & Pfeiffer, Vevey. 50½″ x 37⁷⁄₁₆ (128 x 90 cm). Collection Susan J. Pack.

Arts Décoratifs.) The school, however, did not prove to be much of a financial success. Unlike Paul Colin's school, which took in many students, Cassandre limited the enrollment to around twenty-five students, a small number of whom were allowed to attend free. His major undoing turned out to be his practice of discouraging the ungifted students from continuing and encouraging those he thought had genuine talent. According to André François, the well-known artist and illustrator, students were encouraged to discover special techniques and to work with a limited number of colors, as Cassandre did in his own work. Besides André François, two of France's best-known poster artists of today, Raymond Savignac and Bernard Villemot, also attended the school.

Yet other fields in which Cassandre was to occupy himself were scenery and costume design for the stage. They were an endeavor that would consume more years of steady work than even his poster designing. He began this career in 1933 when he was asked by Louis Jouvet, who had taken over the Théâtre Athenée in Paris, to do the decors for Jean Giraudoux's *Amphytrion 38*. The following year Cassandre designed a production of *Aubade*, with music by Francis Poulenc, for the Ballets Russes de Monte Carlo. By all indications there was a seven-year lapse in his theatre design activities because, in part, of several trips he made between Paris and the United States between 1936 (when The Museum of Modern Art, New York, mounted an exhibition of his posters [15]) and 1939. While in America he did many covers for *Harper's Bazaar* and commissions for the advertising agency N.W. Ayer & Son of Philadelphia. Two of the accounts he worked on were the Ford Motor Company, for which he did his best American poster, *Watch the Fords Go By*, and Dole Pineapple.

With the beginning of World War II in Europe, Cassandre returned to France for good to fulfill his military obligation. More significantly, though, this period marked the beginning of a complete change in his artistic interests and endeavors. He renounced poster and graphic art nearly entirely to concentrate on stage design and easel painting. He had already formed a close friendship with the painter Balthus, who heavily influenced his painting, but, nonetheless, Cassandre never met any financial success in this field

---

(*Opposite*). Cover for *Acier*, a booklet on the uses of steel. 1934. L'Office Technique pour L'Utilisation de L'Acier, Paris. Collection Susan J. Pack.

(*Right*). Deck of playing cards created for Hermès, Paris. 1948. Draeger Frères, Paris. Collection Reinhold-Brown Gallery, New York.

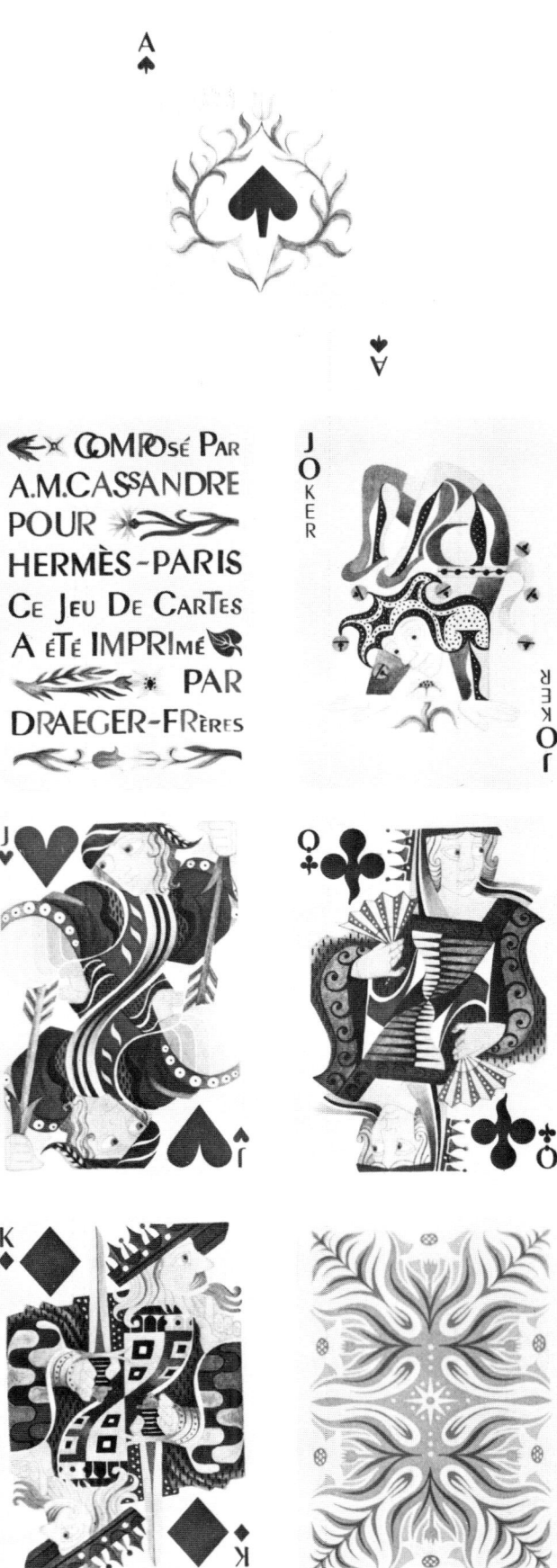

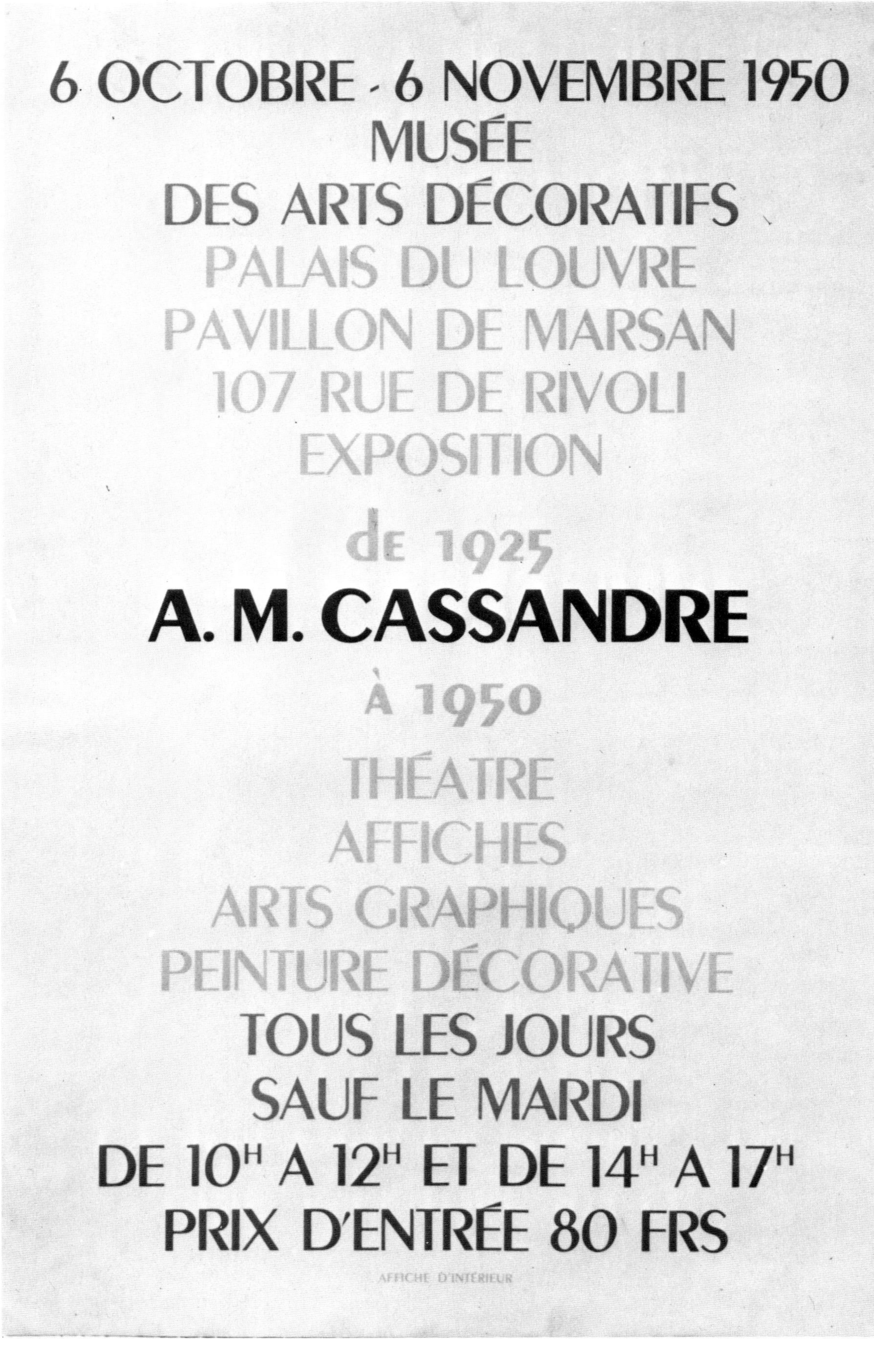

6 OCTOBRE - 6 NOVEMBRE 1950
MUSÉE
DES ARTS DÉCORATIFS
PALAIS DU LOUVRE
PAVILLON DE MARSAN
107 RUE DE RIVOLI
EXPOSITION
DE 1925
A. M. CASSANDRE
À 1950
THÉATRE
AFFICHES
ARTS GRAPHIQUES
PEINTURE DÉCORATIVE
TOUS LES JOURS
SAUF LE MARDI
DE 10ʰ A 12ʰ ET DE 14ʰ A 17ʰ
PRIX D'ENTRÉE 80 FRS

AFFICHE D'INTÉRIEUR

in spite of an exhibition in November 1942 at Galerie René Drouin on Place Vendôme. Still, Cassandre was kept busy with stage design until the mid-1950s, when he began to refuse several commissions. Whereas Cassandre had previously followed developments in modern art, he then began to invoke his own "call to order" in his artistic endeavors by drawing on Quattrocento and Romantic painters and worshiping the music of Mozart; activities that may have had something to do with his receiving a commission from Gabriel Dussurget to design the open-air theatre in Aix-en-Provence (for which Dussurget raised the money in 1947), become its artistic director (a job he resigned in 1951, after only two years, because of the actors' refusal to wear costumes designed by Balthus), and design the sets and costumes for *Don Giovanni*, which were used for almost twenty-five years.

Still, Cassandre could never completely escape from his early success as a poster artist. In 1948 he worked on the previously mentioned monograph, *A. M. Cassandre: Peintre d'Affiches,* published by Zollikofer et Cie of St. Gallen, Switzerland. He also designed at least two posters in the 1940s and three posters in the 1950s (as well as the YSL logotype for Yves St. Laurent in 1963) and had four exhibitions of his posters: at the Musée des Arts Décoratifs in Paris in 1950, at Galerie Motte in Geneva and Galerie Janine Hao in Paris in 1966, and at the Rijksakademie van Beeldende Kunsten in Amsterdam in 1967.

Cassandre's last years were spent in relative poverty and psychological decline. He was hard pressed to earn a living during his last ten years, even though his friends and colleagues thought that the French government should have given him a sinecure with a stipend. When he had his exhibition in Paris in 1966, it was the beginning of the Art Deco revival and many people began to realize that Cassandre was one of France's most important artists. His close friends, the sculptor Raymond Mason and his wife, Janine Hao in whose gallery the exhibition was held, were helpful in finding projects for Cassandre to work on. Unfortunately, because of the student riots in June 1968, these commissions were postponed, a circumstance that contributed to Cassandre's death. Raymond Mason believes that had Cassandre not chosen to take his life, he would have been able to begin working actively again.

(*Opposite*). Exposition A. M. Cassandre. 1950. Publisher not given. 39⅜" x 24⁷⁄₁₆" (100 x 62 cm). Collection Reinhold-Brown Gallery, New York.

(*Above*). Part of the Cassandre exhibition of original artwork at the Galerie Janine Hao, Paris. 1966. Photograph courtesy Raymond Mason and Janine Hao.

III. Cassandre's Style

When discussing posters of the 1920s and 1930s, collectors and scholars of modern applied art often speak of "the Cassandre style." Besides being a term of praise, it also implies the extraordinary talent Cassandre had for the medium. The reasons that Cassandre stood above any other commercial poster artist of the period are numerous. As already mentioned, he had an ability to understand and make use of elements found in avant-garde painting and design and, by so doing, he was able to free postermaking from a long-felt influence of the German designers, the caricaturesque and often-times grotesque influence of Cappiello and other Italian poster designers, as well as from the heavy-handed attempts deriving from a watered-down use of Cubism. Cassandre's talent, however, was based on much more than simply transposing influences. What served him best was his ability to take a theme or subject and create one or more symbols to which he could then give a multidimensionality that often in a single image would evoke a multitude of associations. He was able to do this not by relying on complex realism but by taking the opposite tack and homing in on the most direct and compelling theme and cleverly reconstructing it in an architecturally ingenious fashion that would sometimes go so far as to create a give-and-take relationship between the imagery and the lettering.

The elements of Cassandre's style and the various directions that it took can best be explained by analyzing specific examples of his work. Therefore, we have selected several that appear in the plates that follow.

Plate 2. *Au Bûcheron: le Grand Magasin du Meuble* (1923). In need of a new visual motif, the furniture store Au Bûcheron commissioned Cassandre to design a large poster for the Métro stations. Although it was not the first poster signed "A. M. Cassandre," he considered it his first. It is a good example of the way applied artists of the time used elementary geometric forms such as the step motif and stylized sun rays. Although the poster lacks the sure-handed dynamism one associates with Cassandre's later works, he still saves himself by an appropriate and limited choice of colors, the inherent drama of the motif created by the rippling muscles of the "bûcheron," the cracks and fragments where the tree has been cut, and the pulsating contrast of the white, yellow, and orange of the background. He also takes liberties with reality by moving the potential point of impact of the ax blade to the woodcutter's foot instead of to the base of the tree in order to compose him in relation to the light rays and to show the figure in the most dynamic pose.

Plate 3. *PiVolo* (1924). Executed the year after *Au Bûcheron*, *PiVolo* shows a marked contrast to it. Here Cassandre illustrates the influence of Bernhard and his followers by omitting background detail and playing on a visual pun (a "pie" in French is a magpie). In terms of composition and lettering, though, Cassandre's approach is decidedly French. The wine glass was a widely used motif in synthetic Cubism and Purism, which Cassandre gives a faceted and crystalline quality that one associates with the artists of these movements. The bird is composed entirely of curves and straight lines, a unified approach that became a hallmark in many of his subsequent posters. The lettering is drawn similarly, with interesting decorative characteristics given to the word *PiVolo*. There Cassandre splits the separate elements of each letter, including the space between them, into three different colors and makes use of the ubiquitous disk motif of Léger and Delaunay as the dot above the *i*.

Plate 5. *L'Intransigeant* (1925). Considered by many to be Cassandre's masterpiece, this poster for a Parisian newspaper is certainly one of his most audacious. The primary sources of inspiration are the "papier-collé" works of Braque and Picasso that they made in the period from 1912 to 1914. Although Cassandre did not use cutout paper when making the poster, it nevertheless has that quality because of the incisive way the neck and the face of Marianne, the symbolic voice of France, are outlined against the black background. But the most apparent device used by Cassandre to recall papier-collé is the execution of the lettering. As Braque and Picasso would abbreviate newspaper mastheads by cutting them in two and pasting on one of the pieces, so does Cassandre achieve the same result with printing ink. Coincidentally, he could have eliminated the *s* in "L'Intrans" and have been left with the popular short name of the paper, but in what must have been an audacious move at the time, he did not. In addition, he also shortens the newspaper's caption, "Le Plus Fort Tirage des Journaux de Soir." The poster is also noteworthy because it is the first time that Cassandre uses a "mobile" storytelling device in a single image by depicting the information being transmitted over the telegraph wires, being received through the disklike ear of Marianne, and then being disseminated again through her open mouth.

That *L'Intransigeant* was the most experimental and advanced commercial poster of its time—it was made in a large horizontal format to go on the newspaper's delivery trucks—is also because of the influence of Léger in its conception. The geometrized, almost featureless Marianne is a variation of Léger's anonymous city man that appeared in his paintings from 1918 to 1921. The targetlike eyes that represent Marianne's tricolored ones can also be seen in some of Léger's paintings, most notably in the 1918 *Les Acrobats dans le Cirque,* in which he also used the polelike device off to one side to divide the picture space.[16] This approach to rendering human beings was one that Cassandre would use well into the 1930s, most notably in his posters for Dubonnet. In fact, it wasn't until the 1930s that he would do lifelike portrayals of people and, even then, very infrequently.

Plate 7. *Grand Sport* (c. 1925). The primary influences for the *Grand Sport* poster are Picasso and the Bauhaus painter Oskar Schlemmer. The overall composition of the poster harks back to a 1913 work of Picasso titled *L'Étudiant à la Pipe,*[17] in which the Cubist master depicts a nearly identically modeled *faluche* on the head of a man who is smoking a pipe. However, the way Cassandre drew the head and facial features is derived directly from Schlemmer in its use of simple lines to connote the eyes, ear, and nose. What is most subtle and interesting about the poster is the suggestion of a multiple perspective, which gives a simultaneous straight-on and cocked-to-the-right viewpoint of the face. Cassandre also strengthens the impact of the central image by making a loose outline of the face with an airbrush and extending the interrupted vertical lines from the shoulder to the solid, gray block behind and above the yellow hat.

Plate 8. *Société Anonyme de Gérance et d'Armement* (1927). This poster marks the beginning of Cassandre's most consistent and dynamic period of postermaking, one that lasted until the early 1930s. One might call this period his "expansionistic" phase in that most of his posters for the next four years expanded from the confines of the product poster to the wide spaces of travel posters, even though this particular work is not a travel poster in its literal sense. Here he begins playing with the notion of perspective in a Cubist fashion because the ocean background, which ordinarily should recede in deep perspective, is given only a slight suggestion of recession while the wood crate in the foreground is rendered as a solidly designed and faceted cube. Also this is the first poster in which Cassandre resorts to a prominent distortion of scale by making the crate many times larger, in relation to the ship, than it actually should be, so that he could emphasize the primary activity of the poster's sponsor. The utilization of contrasting forms is also made prominent by changing the color of the support cable from black to white as it reaches the point of juxtaposition with the bow of the ship and the addition of white highlighting in the upper half of the image, a device he may have picked up from Gris's synthetic Cubist paintings of around 1915. Worth noting also is Cassandre's first use of gradation in rendering the sky, a device he would use often between 1927 and 1935.

Plate 9. *Nord Express* (1927). With *Nord Express* Cassandre begins to use vanishing perspective in quite interesting and daring ways. What is so unusual here is that the receding effect takes place in the extreme right corner of the image at a ninety-degree angle that is achieved by making the telegraph wires recede straight back and the locomotive move from left to right. Cassandre integrates the letters into the pictorial matter first by making the split-colored D and the final S carry on the direction of the first telegraph wire and then by fashioning the train's destinations into railway track, part of which carries the rear wheels of the train. Again there is a Légeresque influence on the way Cassandre has modeled the locomotive. Cassandre has idealized it into a smoothly polished array of contrasting light and dark tube and disk formations akin to such Léger paintings as *La Partie des Cartes* (1917).[18] The scale of the locomotive has been rearranged to emphasize the wheels and, by shrinking the body, to give the dynamic streamlining that is central to the overall effect. The end result is one that produces a kinetic, futuristic version of a train without making the viewer think twice about what he is looking at.

Plate 10. *Étoile du Nord* (1927). Of all Cassandre's posters, *Étoile du Nord* may be his most audacious. He has dispensed with the railway imagery that one had always encountered in every previous railway poster: coaches, locomotives, passengers, baggage, conductors, and so forth. Leaving only the rails, Cassandre solves the problem of having to advertise a daytime service that uses a nocturnal image (the North Star) as its name. He achieves his solution by using the somewhat surreal device of turning a night sky into the ground of the poster and having the star hover above it. In what could have been a static arrangement, the rails are laid out so that they imply forward movement. This is done by splitting one rail off from another and having it rejoin another to its left. Even though such an arrangement is mechanically false (as is just about the entire way all of the rails are juxtaposed), it is precisely because of it that the poster attains a dynamic realism more compelling than "reality itself," which is why *Étoile du Nord* is one of Cassandre's best images.

Plate 11. *Nederlandsche Nyverheidsten Tentoonstelling (Nenyto)* (1928). This poster carries forth Cassandre's fascination with the imagery of modern technology. In this particular case it takes on a certain relevance to the concerns of Amédée Ozenfant's and Le Corbusier's magazine, *L'Esprit Nouveau.* Cassandre's design could easily have found a place in the pages of *L'Esprit Nouveau* alongside the photographs of dams, bridges, factories, and grain elevators that were reproduced in 1920 and 1921 as examples of the editors' concern with order, precision, economy, and the modern environment.[19] Rather than disrupt the smooth rendering of the smokestacks, Cassandre cleverly works the brick material into the lettering and makes the text an integral part of the building's shape.

Plate 12. *Statendam* (1928). In the 1924 Salon des Indépendants a painting titled *Boatdeck* by the American artist Gerald Murphy was exhibited.[20] Although this gigantic thirteen-foot painting is lost, the black-and-white photograph that still exists is sufficient evidence that Cassandre saw the painting and borrowed heavily from it in designing the poster for the Statendam. The obvious similarities are seen in a decision to use only the small but very dramatic top deck of a passenger ship, angled smokestacks, funnels, and halyards. Where Cassandre departs from Murphy is in the simplification and distortion of the rendering. Whereas Murphy involves an array of ventilation funnels and wheels in true relative scale, Cassandre draws only two funnels, one of which is rendered nearly the size of the smokestacks. Murphy's painting may be more dramatic and dynamic by virtue of having the smokestacks tower above the architectural elements beneath them, but Cassandre's poster, with its experiment in playing with scale, is certainly more unorthodox.

Plate 13. *LMS Bestway* (1928). In terms of its image and the energy it connotes, *LMS Bestway* is Cassandre's most powerful poster. By changing to the unusual nearly square format, he evokes a feeling of vertical and horizontal compression of energy about to be unleashed. As in *Nord Express*, Cassandre uses a variety of contrasts and geometric forms to express and evoke the turning of the train wheels and driving rods that are not much more than blurs of gray and white. The notion of speed is best realized by the manner in which he juxtaposes the splitting of the disks into disproportionate black-and-white sections and the way that he makes one large wheel black and the other a gradation of white, gray, and black. By leaving the area above the wheels relatively flat and solid and creating an artful cacophony of light, shading, and geometric forms, he is able to emphasize the kinetic and dynamic aspects of a train in motion. In certain respects, *LMS Bestway* fits into a body of machine art that was done by Léger, Willi Baumeister, and the Belgian Victor Servranckx to whose painting *Opus 47* (1923) this poster bears a resemblance.

Plate 14. *Écosse (par les trains deluxe LMS)* (1928). How attentive and facile Cassandre was as a poster designer is vividly illustrated in this work. Without warning, he switches from the realm of the geometric abstract painting of the 1910s and early 1920s to the looser or curvilinear Cubism that was practiced by Braque, Picasso, Auguste Herbin, and others. The splitting of objects into contrasting light and dark areas was a device used mostly by Braque throughout the 1920s. Cassandre still introduces some strictly linear forms into the poster, but he contrasts them with more graceful and naturalistic ones as well. By dispensing with a uniform border and heightening the area between this irregular margin with a meandering highlighting, he creates a fragmented landscape that looks as though it has been cut out and pasted on. The poster shows another artful use of contrast, but this time he creates a unified image by reconciling seemingly opposed shapes.

Plate 19. *La Route Bleue* (1929). One of Cassandre's most direct and architecturally constructed posters, *La Route Bleue*'s major motif consists of two pairs of converging acute triangles that are joined by increasingly smaller rectangles. Loosely jagged white lines are then superimposed in near-random fashion as foliage for these purely geometric trees. This foliage device was borrowed three years later by a designer no less great than Herbert Bayer for his poster *Die Strasse*. As a subtle visual pun, Cassandre makes the

---

Gerald Murphy: *Boatdeck*. 1923. Oil on canvas, 156″ x 105″ (396 x 266.5 cm). Photograph courtesy Mrs. William Donnelly.

Victor Servranckx: *Opus 47*. 1923. Oil on canvas, 40½" x 82" (102.8 x 208 cm). Collection Musée Royaux des Beaux-Arts de Belgique, Brussels.

border olive green to suggest the olive trees of Provence, which is where the buses being advertised passed through on their way to the Côte d'Azur.

Plate 21. *R.A.I. Automobiel- & Motorrijwiel Tentoonstelling* (designed 1929). Even with a subject with as long a pedigree in poster art as the automobile show, Cassandre still finds a way to present it in an innovative fashion. Instead of focusing only on a display, he makes the visitor an integral part of the poster, not as a passive onlooker dwarfed by the exhibits but as one whose fascination is larger than the automobile itself. Again Cassandre uses a split image by dividing the grille into two colors as well as leaving out the entire right side of the automobile. The left side, meanwhile, is supported by *RAI*, the initials for the building in which the show was held.

Plate 22. *Champions du Monde* (1930). After a period of rendering mobile, dynamic, and large-scale subjects, Cassandre at the beginning of the 1930s begins as often as not to design posters in which the subjects become larger than life. *Champions du Monde* is a good example of this. Whereas Cassandre was formerly interested in contrasts of form, he now also concerns himself with contrasts of light by using a nocturnal lighting effect (a Surrealist concern used very early on in this poster) that is juxtaposed by a seemingly spotlighted book. The fingers are modeled in the large, hefty, fashion that Cassandre would use several times in the future. *Champions du Monde* has such a photographic quality that one can only marvel at how well it would stand up to today's superrealist paintings. After all, this poster, devoid of any typographical message, is a lithographed version of one of these paintings.

Plate 23. *Dr. Charpy* (1930). The notion that a young, beautiful face has certain elements of balance, symmetry, and proportion that can be enhanced by patronizing the products of Dr. Charpy is the subtle theme of this intelligent and rather complex poster. The "before and after" theme is deftly handled by making the right side of the face a somber, black image in a mirror in need of the color and definition promised by the left side. The rendering of the face is Matisse-like, while the use of the anonymous artstore stencil lettering (abandoned in the printed version) comes from Le Corbusier. In fact, the idea of sectioning off the left side of the face recalls the drawing in of golden section triangles in some of Corbusier's Purist paintings of 1920 and 1921.

Plate 25. *Triplex* (designed 1930). Here Cassandre turns to a minimalist sort of rendering for a manufacturer of truck safety glass. The only elements are those that are absolutely essential to put across the message that Triplex makes windshields for trucks; the design eliminates all features of the truckdriver's face except the most relevant one—the eyes; the only grips on the steering wheel are those between the hands; and, in the most ingenious part of the poster, a small but well-defined sheet of glass hovers "illogically" in space with the Triplex trademark clearly

Preliminary gouache study for *Triplex*. 1929. 26″ x 20½″ (66 x 52 cm). Collection Barry Friedman, Ltd., New York.

---

visible in its proper scale. Certainly any other poster designer would most probably have tried the more obvious and less elegant approach of drawing the entire front of a truck cab.

Plate 27. *En Wagons-Lits* (1930). In one of Cassandre's most haunting and simple posters, he again takes an unconventional approach. He resists the notion that a travel poster has to be bright, colorful, and entirely legible at a glance. Once more he eschews the conventional imagery that would have called for a sleeping car, in favor of a primary image that a sleeping car passenger never sees; a railway traffic signal in the middle of night. In rendering it, Cassandre deftly plays with circles. A yellow disk is enclosed by an orange glow, part of which has been made into a disk by a very thin black circle. This arrangement is then placed down and right of center of the large black circle that forms the fixture on the top of the tower. As the final touch, all of these elements are then surrounded by a halo of blue light. To emphasize that this array of circles was well thought out, Cassandre carries the circle motif into the lettering by ingeniously enclosing the top of the 2.

Plate 28. *Heemaf* (1930). In this poster for a Dutch electrical company, Cassandre evokes a Dadaistic concern with machinery and mechanization; specifically Francis Picabia's painting *Machine Tournez Vite* (1916-1917).[21] Picabia's painting of turning gears was done with a sense of parody, and it seems that Cassandre found some inspiration in it, because he also brings in specific electromechanical elements without drawing an identifiable machine. A lightning bolt represents a spark jumping between positive and negative poles and its response is measured by a randomly placed, near-parody of an electrometer. The meshing of the gears is emphasized by making the teeth appear in only a part of the two wheels and, once again, as he did in *L'Intransigeant,* Cassandre finds it sufficient to use only enough letters, "voor el," to make the point that Heemaf is "for electricity."

Plate 29. *Spidoléine* (1931). Even in a poster as spare as *Spidoléine*, there is still plenty of room for playfulness. The natural inclination would have been to take a relatively small object—in this case a can of oil—and make it life size or larger. Here Cassandre makes a more effective advertisement by taking the completely opposite approach of shrinking the oilcan's size. Instead of re-creating the lettering on the oilcan, he turns instead to a typographic exercise by extending the letters beyond the limits of the object and progressively diminishing the size of the characters while switching their color from yellow to black as they intrude on the yellow band. Cassandre also uses what for him is an unusually large number of colors (four), but the red and the blue are used so sparingly that they achieve maximum impact. Finally, the one-word message, *Securité*, is joined to the central image by a descending line from the spout of the oilcan.

Plate 31. *L'Atlantique* (1931). In this passenger ship poster, Cassandre gives a different sort of dynamic quality to a ponderous steamship, as he does to a speeding streamlined train. He achieves this by once more resorting to the distortion-of-scale device that by 1931 had become a major weapon in his arsenal. Instead of "a sleek oceangoing vessel," as writers often describe modern ships, Cassandre's rendition becomes a mammoth wall of steel that towers in fantastic and unreal fashion over a minuscule tugboat. He further adds to this startling effect by collapsing the upper decks and the three smokestacks so that they appear almost flat. Cassandre also distorts perspective in an ingenious way; the stern of the ship extends into the front of the top decks as well as down from them (along with the bow) into the ocean to form a reflection. When taken together, all of these elements, along with the block of text, form one awesome rectangular shape that passes through a "wreath" formed by the coming together of the smoke from the tugboat and the steamship.

Plate 32. *S.S. Côte d'Azur* (1931). Without resorting to any obvious visual sleight of hand, Cassandre presents a rather conventional rendition, at least in comparison to *L'Atlantique*, of a steamship. By contrast he takes the approach of limiting the image to a concentrated side view. Nonetheless, he has selected the most formally interesting area of the small cross-channel ship and is thus able to bring into play the variety of shapes in the smokestack, funnel, railing, the lifeboat and its support, and the ship's one deck. Once more he invokes the steam/smoke motif that appears in many of his posters by contrasting black smoke with white clouds. The way in which he has the black hull serve a dual purpose by acting as the background for the lettering is clever enough, but he carries it one step further by enclosing the words "*Côte d'Azur*" in quotation marks that also serve as four small portholes.

Plate 34. *Wagon-Bar* (1932). In contrast to his previous masterful railroad posters, Cassandre concerns himself with a static composition that draws on Purist still lifes and the photomontage experiments of the Bauhaus and the Russian Constructivists. One needs only to look at the early 1920s paintings of Ozenfant and Le Corbusier, which illustrated their doctrine of Purism. In formulating it, they set down a series of principles based on mathematical and structural order, reason, and precision that resulted in various hierarchies of color, form, and subject matter. Practically speaking, the end results, in simplistic terms, were canvases whose colors fell into the so-called great scale—"ochres, reds, earth colors, white, black, and ultramarine-colors which promoted unity because they neither appeared to advance nor to retreat" [22]—and whose subject matter consisted of "type objects" (guitars, wine bottles, glasses, and so forth) whose "perfect simplicity . . . and their relationship with man were symbolic of an all-embracing idea of the principles governing order in life." [23] The still-life objects, therefore, that most conformed to the ideals of Purism were those that attained a pure perfection, which is why Purist paintings show objects that are considered to be timeless. That *Wagon-Bar* can be considered nearly a Purist poster is evidenced by the grouping of the wine and water glasses, the loaf of bread, the siphon, and the wine bottles—the colors of which fall into the Purists' "great scale."

Photomontage was an approach that Cassandre had avoided until *Wagon-Bar*. That he followed developments related or pertaining to it is confirmed by the fact that Cassandre selected several examples for a book on international advertising published in 1929.[24] Although photomontage was a medium he never became very fond of, Cassandre shows here that he was able to use it most cleverly and effectively, as is evidenced by the way he superimposes the still life over the train wheel and his making a gracefully balanced structure of the short piece of track and the three rows of lettering.

Plate 35. *Pathé: l'Enregistrement Électrique le Plus Perfectionné* (1932). As in *Champions du Monde*, Cassandre creates a Surrealist contrast of light on a subject made larger than life. He extends the light effect by cleverly curving the slogan around the edge of the phonograph record so that the word *électrique* falls into the bright light. The enormous scale of the phonograph record is made even greater by cutting nearly half of it off with the left margin. Although the overall effect borders on the eerie, *Pathé* attains a rare elegant simplicity.

Plate 37. *Dubo . . . Dubon . . . Dubonnet* (1932). Among French posters of the twentieth century none is better known among Frenchmen than *Dubo . . . Dubon . . . Dubonnet*. It was kept in circulation for more than two decades and issued in a variety of formats so that it could be used on billboards, in the Métro tunnels, on writing pads given out on the railroads, and so forth. Whether or not Cassandre was thinking of comic strips or motion pictures is impossible to say, but in any case this Dubonnet poster is his most overtly witty. The slogan is a pun using the words *dubo* (doubt), *du bon* (good), and *Dubonnet*. In the first panel of the triptych, the Dubonnet man eyes the glass with suspicion, and color is added to the parts of him that are involved in this sizing-up process. As the design moves along, more color is added until the contented man and his table are completely filled in as he pours his second glass. In relation to his other great posters, *Dubo . . . Dubon . . . Dubonnet* seems like a radical departure, but in fact it retains some already familiar approaches. For example, he plays with the nonimage elements that involve not only the play on words but the border. Instead of putting the matching colored edges opposite one another, he puts them at right angles. He still distorts scale—not as obviously, but just as effectively —by enlarging the Dubonnet man's eye, which he uses most efficiently by changing the position of the eyeball in the middle section. He also uses color gradation in the background that not only heightens the impact of what is taking place but also serves as a smooth transition and framing device between the three panels.

Plate 39. *Grande Quinzaine Internationale de Lawn-Tennis* (1932). Yet another fine example of Cassandre's simple-yet-subtle style, this poster abounds in interesting visual effects. Put in cinematic terms, Cassandre juxtaposes a close-up with a long shot by having the tennis ball hurtling through space toward the spectator while diminishing the scale of the tennis player by keeping him well in the background. Certain seemingly important details such as strands in the net and the seam on the tennis ball—not to mention the player himself who is represented only as a solid, featureless form—are dispensed with. Airbrushed black and white around the tennis ball create the interesting effect of lightening and darkening each component of the image: ball, net, player, and center line.

Plate 40. *Le Jour* (1933). Never one to stand still or become burdened by any single approach, Cassandre shows new concerns and directions in this poster for a soon-to-be-published newspaper. At first glance, the poster looks like nothing more than two contrasting areas that signify day and night. However, a longer look at the large yellow form shows that it is a flattened rendering of France with two small clouds placed diagonally across from each other. The nocturnal section of the poster, part of which is unobtrusively formed to pass through the globe to form the darkened half of the earth, shows Cassandre's concern with the biomorphic forms of Arp and Miró. *Le Jour* is one of Cassandre's most successful attempts at using and manipulating symbols in a multifaceted way while showing that he could be as adept at using a surreal and curvilinear approach as he could a Cubist or geometric one.

Plate 47. *Maison Prunier* (1934). Throughout the 1920s, Georges Braque painted scores of tabletops laden with food. They were clearly an inspiration behind this poster for Prunier's in London. Although Cassandre's design is a much simpler version, without the nearly overhead perspective and the full array of food that marked Braque's work, he borrows the technique (as he did in *Écosse*) of dividing a motif (in this case the fish) into two contrasting colors. What is unique about *Maison Prunier* is the way that Cassandre avoids the cliché of presenting a realistically set table in favor of limiting himself to just the key symbols of a seafood restaurant (including the rather unorthodox but relevant seashell), which he places in random space on and above the table. A rather traditional use of chiaroscuro is also effective in giving the table legs and cloth a feeling of solidity.

Plate 49. *Pernod Fils* (1934). A more deft and witty use of photomontage is difficult to find in posters of this period. The photograph of a smiling, moustachioed man is used to fuse the elements of man, glass, and bottle together into a clever and surreal poster design. The photograph has been divided into three elements: first, by the white line that indicates the level of the absinthe, whose yellow color has been lightly applied over part of the face, and second, by the edge of the green bottle that covers the left side of the face. Subtle effects of light, texture, and color gradation are achieved by painting over the photograph while the letters are playfully curved to imply a continuation of the edge of the glass.

Plate 50. *Sweepstake: Prix de l'Arc de Triomphe* (1935). The drama and excitement of a photo finish are stirringly depicted by the concentrated and overlapping form of two jockeys and horses crossing a finish line. By flattening and combining the two jockeys, so that their silks are joined together, that the riding boots of one jockey are placed directly behind those of the other, and that the color of one horse switches from black to brown, Cassandre evokes the feeling of blurred, blinding speed that is always associated with the neck-and-neck battle of a stretch run. As in *L'Intransigeant*, Cassandre splits the picture frame with a pole device, only this time he establishes its width from the letter *E* beneath it and brings it into play as the finishing line of the race.

Plate 51. *Nicolas* (1935). The *Nicolas* poster was designed to be printed in an enormous size (320 x 240 cm or 126″ x 94½″). In this version a light blue-, brown-, and white-striped border was added.[25] Although rarely seen in its full glory, the chromatic, vibrant, and pulsating aspects were still effective in its trimmed, cut-down car-card size. The figure carrying the bottles was originally created for Nicolas by Dransy around 1920 and given the name of Nectar. The character quickly assumed a popularity among children and adults that turned him into a French institution.

The basis for the poster's startling pattern effect are the bottles that appear to be both swirling and stationary. They provide the thrust for the circular motif of the red, yellow, and orange stripes that collide and refract off one another. Some have said that this effect was a precursor of the Op art of the 1960s; a statement that is not really correct as there are no optical effects. Rather, it bears a closer resemblance to Robert Delaunay's simultanism, twenty years prior to the Nicolas poster. Regardless, Cassandre creates an interesting effect by changing the color, direction, and alignment of the stripes and sectioning them off into a triangle and irregular rectangles, as well as having them blend into the biomorphic form he uses as the ground for the *Nicolas* poster. Also worth noting is the light and shadow effect that appears to have as its source the triangle that begins above the lower-right corner and dissipates as it hits the circle surrounding the yellow bottles.

Plate 53. *Normandie* (1935). Often regarded as one of Cassandre's strongest and most elegant posters of his "classic" style, *Normandie* is still as much an example of his work in the 1930s as of the 1920s. Unlike *L'Atlantique*, to which this poster bears some resemblance because of the elongated bow and the compressed top deck, Cassandre releases some of the tension that the earlier poster had by slightly curving his lines, especially in the white areas above the hull. This creates somewhat of a drooping effect that one does not see in his earlier work. However, he does, almost as a last gasp, retain two earlier devices: that of gradating the sky and the hull and aligning the bottom of the stern with the starting and ending points of the word *Normandie*. Although it is unusual to see so much text in a Cassandre poster, he minimizes the intrusion by keeping it below the image and in a discreet scale.

Although the years 1927 to 1932 are considered to be Cassandre's most prodigious period of poster design, it would not be quite accurate to say that his talents ebbed in the years that followed. In retrospect, the posters that were produced between *Nord Express* and *Dubo . . . Dubon . . . Dubonnet* do constitute his most exciting body of work. In the overall view, however, his output from 1924 to 1939 closely follows, in delayed fashion, the developments in modern French art: synthetic and analytic Cubism, Dada, Purism, Machine art, later Cubism, Surrealism, and the classicizing tendencies of the early 1920s. For Cassandre to have designed a poster such as *L'Intransigeant* or *Nord Express* in the mid- or late 1930s would have been regarded by Cassandre as rather passé, if not slightly bizarre. The fact is that Cassandre was unlike the majority of postermakers, who turned out designs in a haphazard or unenlightened fashion. His artistic development was that of a fine painter who indulges in experimentation and is always moving forward into new territory.

IV. Posterography: 1922–1939

The following is a listing of A. M. Cassandre's posters executed between 1922 and 1939. The sources for it are books and periodicals that reproduced photographs of Cassandre's work and posters that are in the collections of museums, dealers, and collectors. Although it is nearly inevitable that obscure or unknown Cassandre posters will come to light in the ensuing years, this list, which comprises 117 entries, is virtually definitive, especially in light of the fact that it has been previously stated that Cassandre designed "about 100" posters. In several instances, especially with his earliest posters, we could not always give the precise year that the posters were designed, either because he did not date all of his posters or because the date was illegible in the magazine reproductions that were sometimes our only source of documentation. Uncertainties and omissions regarding dates and publishers could have been rectified had we been able to have all the original specimens at our disposal.

This posterography does not include those posters that were reprinted with varying margins or text, working designs that were not printed, or any posters that were signed as studio pieces or as being "after" A. M. Cassandre. For reasons of space, we did not include every source in which a poster was found, but rather restricted the citation to the most readily available book or periodical.

The plate number refers only to the color illustrations in this book.

REFERENCES CITED:

Zollikofer: *A. M. Cassandre: peintre d'affiches*. St. Gallen: Zollikofer et Cie, 1948.
AMG: *Arts et Métiers Graphiques*, Paris (1927–1939).
CAI: *Commercial Art & Industry*, London (1922–1936).
Vendre: *Vendre*, Paris (1923–).
Gebr.: *Gebrauchsgraphik*, Berlin (1925–).

1. *Sadac*. 1922. Hachard & Cie, Paris. **Plate 1.**
2. *À Moi les Vraies Pâtes Garres*. c. 1922. Hachard & Cie, Paris. *Gebr.*, June 1927, p. 47.
3. *Au Bûcheron: le Grand Magasin du Meuble*. 1923. Hachard & Cie, Paris. **Plate 2.**
4. *PiVolo*. 1924. Hachard & Cie, Paris. **Plate 3.**
5. *Onoto*. c. 1924. Hachard & Cie, Paris. *L'Art Vivant*, November 15, 1926, p. 855.
6. *Le Nouvelliste: C'est l'Ordre*. c. 1924. Hachard & Cie, Paris. *Posters & Publicity*, 1927, p. 62.
7. *Turmac: la Cigarette Turque*. c. 1924. Hachard & Cie, Paris. *Gebr.*, June 1927, p. 47.
8. *Cycles Brillant*. c. 1924. Hachard & Cie, Paris. Copy in the collection of Galerie Gerard, New York.
9. *PiVolo: Aperitif aux Vins de France*. c. 1924. Hachard & Cie, Paris. *Gebr.*, June 1927, p. 47.
10. *Réglisse Florent*. 1925. Hachard & Cie, Paris. **Plate 4.**
11. *L'Intransigeant*. 1925. Hachard & Cie, Paris. **Plate 5.**
12. *Huile de la Croix Verte*. 1925. Hachard & Cie, Paris. *L'Art Vivant*, November 15, 1926, p. 855.
13. *Au Bûcheron: Grand Prix de l'Ensemble de l'Exposition Internationale des Arts Décoratifs*. 1925. Hachard & Cie, Paris. *Gebr.*, June 1927, p. 47.
14. *Le Kid: Vaporisateur de Poche Indispensable*. c. 1925. Hachard & Cie, Paris. *Gebr.*, June 1927, p. 47.

15. *Golden Club.* c. 1925. Hachard & Cie, Paris. **Plate 6.**
16. *Grand Sport: le Casquette Adoptée par Tous les Champions.* c. 1925. Hachard & Cie, Paris. **Plate 7.**
17. *Thiery Aîné & Cie.* c. 1925. Hachard & Cie, Paris. *Gebr.,* June 1927, p. 47.
18. *Aéro-Club de Bourgogne.* c. 1925. Hachard & Cie, Paris. *Gebr.,* June 1927, p. 47.
19. *Huilor.* c. 1925. Hachard & Cie, Paris. *Vendre,* June 1925, p. 623.
20. *Huilor* (another version). c. 1925. Hachard & Cie, Paris. *Vendre,* September 1926, p. 224.
21. *Exposition de la Photographie et du Cinéma.* 1926. Hachard & Cie, Paris. *Vendre,* March 1926, p. 280.
22. *Sools: Maître Chapelier.* 1926. Hachard & Cie, Paris. Zollikofer, p. 18.
23. *Château de la Roche Vasouy.* 1926. Hachard & Cie, Paris. *Gebr.,* June 1927, p. 47.
24. *À la Maison Dorée.* c. 1926. Hachard & Cie, Paris. *Gebr.,* June 1927, p. 47.
25. *À la Maison Dorée* (another version). c. 1926. Hachard & Cie, Paris. *Vendre,* February 1927, p. 188.
26. *Société Anonyme de Gérance et d'Armement.* 1927. Hachard & Cie, Paris. **Plate 8.**
27. *Nord Express.* 1927. Hachard & Cie, Paris. **Plate 9.**
28. *Étoile du Nord.* 1927. Hachard & Cie, Paris. **Plate 10.**
29. *Le Progres: le Journal de Lyon.* 1927. Hachard & Cie, Paris. *CAI,* January 1928, p. 20.
30. *Emsa: macht die Strümpfe neu und dauerhaft.* c. 1927. Hachard & Cie, Paris. *CAI,* January 1928, p. 22.
31. *Fizz: le Nouveau Vaporisateur.* c. 1927. Hachard & Cie (?), Paris. *Vendre,* March 1928, p. 275.
32. *Nederlandsche Nyverheidsten Tentoonstelling (Nenyto).* 1928. Nijgh en Van Ditmar, Rotterdam. **Plate 11.**
33. *Statendam.* 1928. Nijgh en Van Ditmar, Rotterdam. **Plate 12.**
34. *LMS Bestway.* 1928. McCorquodale & Co., Ltd., London. **Plate 13.**
35. *Écosse (par les trains deluxe LMS).* 1928. Bemrose & Sons Co., Ltd., Derby. **Plate 14.**
36. *LMS The Best Way* (or *LMS Grande Bretagne*). 1928. L. Danel, Lille. **Plate 15.**
37. *Goedkoope Biljetten naar Londen.* 1928. Nijgh en Van Ditmar (?), Rotterdam. **Plate 16.**
38. *The Continent via Harwich: Day and Night Service.* 1928. Nijgh en Van Ditmar (?), Rotterdam. *CAI,* July 1928, p. 15.
39. *Vu: Illustré de la Semaine.* 1928. Publisher not given. Zollikofer, p. 28.
40. *Galeries Lafayette: J'achete Tout Aux.* 1928 Galeries Lafayette, Paris. Zollikofer, p. 30.
41. *Galeries Lafayette: J'achete Tout Aux* (photomontage). c. 1928. Galeries Lafayette (?), Paris. *AMG,* no. 7, opp. p. 47.
42. *Galeries Lafayette: Toilettes d'Été.* 1929. Galeries Lafayette, Paris. Zollikofer, p. 31.
43. *Sools: Maître Chapelier.* 1929. Cie Artistique de Publicité, Paris. **Plate 17.**
44. *Chemin de Fer du Nord.* 1929. L. Danel, Lille. **Plate 18.**
45. *La Route Bleue.* 1929. L. Danel, Lille. **Plate 19.**
46. *L'Oiseau Bleu.* 1929. L. Danel, Lille. **Plate 20.**
47. *R.A.I. Automobiel- & Motorrijwiel Tentoonstelling.* Designed 1929. Nijgh en Van Ditmar, Rotterdam. **Plate 21.**
48. *United States Line: London-Paris-Bremen.* c. 1929. Publisher not given. *Gebr.,* July 1929, p. 33.
49. *Droste's (Verpleegster Cacao).* c. 1929. Publisher not given.
50. *Champions du Monde.* 1930. B. Grasset, Paris. **Plate 22.**
51. *Dr. Charpy.* 1930. Cie Artistique de Publicité, Paris. **Plate 23.** Also Zollikofer, p. 39, for the published version.
52. *DeVries Robbe & Company.* 1930. Nijgh en Van Ditmar, Rotterdam. Zollikofer, p. 40.
53. *Lys Chantilly.* 1930. L. Danel, Lille. **Plate 24.**
54. *Triplex.* Designed 1930. Alliance Graphique, Paris. **Plate 25.**
55. *Flèche d'Argent: Aéropostale.* 1930. Société Anonyme Courbet, Paris. **Plate 26.**
56. *En Wagons-Lit.* 1930. L. Danel, Lille. **Plate 27.**
57. *Heemaf.* 1930. Nijgh en Van Ditmar, Rotterdam. **Plate 28.**
58. *Stork-Hijsch: Kranen Transportwerktuigen.* 1930. Nijgh en Van Ditmar, Rotterdam. Zollikofer, p. 44.
59. *BK Emaille.* 1930. Alliance Graphique(?), Paris. Copy in the Stedelijk Museum, Amsterdam.
60. *Veramint de Ricqlès.* 1930. Alliance Graphique(?), Paris. *Gebr.,* January 1933, p. 4.
61. *Vinay Chocolates.* 1930. Les Belles Affiches, Paris. *Gebr.,* September 1930, p. 46.
62. *Paris Films: le Quotidien du Cinéma.* 1931. Alliance Graphique, Paris. Zollikofer, p. 46.
63. *Paris Films.* 1931. Alliance Graphique, Paris. *Vendre,* May 1931, p. 401. A decorative typographic poster designed to accompany the preceding poster.
64. *Van Nelle Pakjes Koffie.* 1931. Nijgh en Van Ditmar, Rotterdam. Zollikofer, p. 47.
65. *Spidoléine.* 1931. Alliance Graphique, Paris. **Plate 29.**
66. *Thomson: La Main-d'Oeuvre Électro-Domestique.* 1931. Alliance Graphique, Paris. **Plate 30.**

67. *L'Atlantique*. 1931. Alliance Graphique, Paris. **Plate 31.**
68. *S.S. Côte d'Azur*. 1931. Alliance Graphique, Paris. **Plate 32.**
69. *Grand Sport: la Casquette Adoptée par Tous les Champions* (another version). 1931. Alliance Graphique, Paris. *Zollikofer*, p. 53.
70. *Miniwatt: Philips Radio*. 1931. Alliance Graphique, Paris. **Plate 33.**
71. *Casino: Je Suis Partout/ Je Vends de Tout*. 1931. Alliance Graphique, Paris. *Zollikofer*, p. 55.
72. *Wagon-Bar*. 1932. L. Danel, Lille. **Plate 34.**
73. *Pathé: L'Enregistrement Électrique le Plus Perfectionné*. 1932. Alliance Graphique, Paris. **Plate 35.**
74. *Pathé. TSF*. 1932. Alliance Graphique(?), Paris. Copy in the Stedelijk Museum, Amsterdam.
75. *Orange: Huile pour Automobiles et Avions*. 1932. Alliance Graphique(?), Paris. *CAI*, May 1933, p. 207.
76. Lettering poster for Dubonnet. 1932. Alliance Graphique, Paris. *Zollikofer*, p. 64.
77. *Air Orient*. 1932. Publisher not given. **Plate 36.**
78. *Dubo . . . Dubon . . . Dubonnet*. 1932. Alliance Graphique, Paris. **Plate 37.**
79. *Unic: Chaussures d'Hommes*. 1932. Alliance Graphique, Paris. **Plate 38.**
80. *Grand Quinzaine Internationale de Lawn-Tennis* (also issued as *Coupe Davis* [*Challenge-Round de la*]). 1932. Alliance Graphique, Paris. **Plate 39.**
81. *Pathé* (*les Meilleurs Postes sont Fabriqué par*). c. 1932. Alliance Graphique(?), Paris. *AMG*, no. 33, January 15, 1933, p. 49.
82. *Le Jour*. 1933. Le Jour, Paris. **Plate 40.**
83. *Roquefort de la Société Agricole*. 1933. Alliance Graphique, Paris. *Zollikofer*, p. 72.
84. *Bonal: la Clef de l'Appetit*. 1933. Alliance Graphique, Paris. *Zollikofer*, p. 75.
85. *Wagons Lits Cook*. 1933. Alliance Graphique, Paris. **Plate 41.**
86. *. . . Mais le Lait est Plus Sain . . .* 1933. Alliance Graphique, Paris. *Zollikofer*, p. 78.
87. *Leroy*. 1933. Alliance Graphique, Paris. **Plate 42.**
88. *Ier Salon de la Qualité Française*. c. 1933. Alliance Graphique(?), Paris. *AMG*, no. 38, November 15, 1933, p. 63.
89. *Écosse*. 1934. Alliance Graphique, Paris. *Zollikofer*, p. 82.
90. *Angleterre*. 1934. Alliance Graphique, Paris. **Plate 43.**
91. *Price's Motorine*. 1934. Price's Motorine, London. **Plate 44.**
92. *Celtique Caporal Ordinaire*. 1934. Alliance Graphique, Paris. **Plate 45.**
93. *Grandes Fêtes de Paris*. 1934. Alliance Graphique, Paris. **Plate 46.**
94. *Maison Prunier*. 1934. Alliance Graphique, Paris. **Plate 47.**
95. *À L'Eau avec un Peu de Cassis ou un Zeste de Citron* (Dubonnet). 1934. Alliance Graphique, Paris. **Plate 48.**
96. *Pernod Fils*. 1934. Alliance Graphique, Paris. **Plate 49.**
97. *Sec. Vin Tonique au Quinquina* (Dubonnet). 1935. Alliance Graphique, Paris. *Zollikofer*, p. 95.
98. *Sweepstake: Prix de l'Arc de Triomphe*. 1935. Alliance Graphique, Paris. **Plate 50.**
99. *Nicolas*. 1935. Alliance Graphique, Paris. **Plate 51.**
100. *Fêtes de Paris*. 1935. Alliance Graphique, Paris. **Plate 52.**
101. *Normandie*. 1935. Alliance Graphique, Paris. **Plate 53.**
102. *Paris*. 1935. Draeger Frères, Paris. **Plate 54.**
103. *Price's Motorine* (another version). Price's Motorine(?), London. *Gebr.*, March 1937, p. 32.
104. *Pacific Cigarettes*. 1935. Säuberlin & Pfeiffer, S.A., Vevey. **Plate 55.**
105. *Tabac Kisroul*. 1935. Säuberlin & Pfeiffer, S.A., Vevey. Copy in the Kunstgewerbemuseum, Zürich.
106. *Vautier César*. 1935. Vautier Frères, S.A., Yverdon. **Plate 56.**
107. *Kina Nectar*. 1936. Draeger Frères, Paris. **Plate 57.**
108. *Decorators Picture Gallery*. 1936. Publisher not given (only one specimen printed). *Zollikofer*, p. 110.
109. *Italia*. 1936. Officina Grafiche Coen & Cia, Milan. **Plate 58.**
110. *Italia* (another version). 1936. Officina Grafiche Coen & Cia, Milan. **Plate 59.**
111. *Italia-Cosulich*. 1936. Officina Grafiche Coen & Cia, Milan. **Plate 60.**
112. *Le Simca Cinq ne Coûte que 9.900 Fr*. 1936. Draeger Imp., Paris. Copy in the collection of Hubert Lemaire, Paris.
113. *Watch the Fords Go By*. 1937. N.W. Ayer & Son, Philadelphia. *Zollikofer*, p. 111.
114. *Dole Pineapple Gems*. 1937. N.W. Ayer & Son, Philadelphia. *Zollikofer*, p. 114.
115. *Colomba Motta*. 1938. Officina Grafiche Coen & Cia, Milan. Copy formerly in the collection of Reinhold-Brown Gallery, New York.
116. *Ambre Solaire*. 1939. Publisher not given. Paris. *Vendre*, August 1938, p. 385.
117. *Sensation Cigarettes*. 1939. Publisher not given. Poster published in the United States. Copy in the Stedelijk Museum, Amsterdam.

NOTES

1. Mildred Constantine and Alan M. Fern. *Word and Image: Posters from the Collection of The Museum of Modern Art* (New York: The Museum of Modern Art, 1968), pp. 12–16.
2. See *Das Frühe Plakat in Europa und den USA*. Vol. 1. Grossbritannien und Vereinigte Staaten von Nordamerika (Berlin: Gebrüder Mann Verlag, 1973), pp. 4–7, for illustrations and descriptions of the Beggarstaffs' posters.
3. Related to us by Bernhard's son, Karl, who is a graphic designer in Levittown, New York.
4. Christopher Green, *Léger and the Avant-Garde* (New Haven and London: Yale University Press, 1976), p. 79.
5. For a detailed and profound study of the literary and artistic avant-garde in Paris during the 1910s and 1920s, see Green, *Léger and the Avant-Garde*.
6. "Art and Poster Art by A. M. Cassandre," *Gebrauchsgraphik* (January 1933), p. 5.
7. A. M. Cassandre, "L'Age de L'Affiche," *L'Affiche Illustré*, Collection Comoedia-Charpentier (Paris: Les Publications Techniques, 1944), p. 3.
8. *A. M. Cassandre: Peintre d'Affiches* (St. Gallen: Zollikofer & Cie, 1948), p. 9.
9. *A. M. Cassandre* (Amsterdam: Rijksakademie van Beeldende Kunsten, 1967), p. 6.
10. Charles Peignot, "Cassandre et la Typographie," *Médecine de France* (January 1969), p. 38.
11. Joseph Blumenthal, "Cassandre's 'Peignot,'" *PM* (October 1937), p. 2.
12. *Ibid.*, p. 4.
13. *A. M. Cassandre: Peintre d'Affiches*, p. 12.
14. Charles Peignot, "Maurice Moyrand est Mort," *Arts et Métiers Graphiques*, no. 43 (October 1934), p. 60.
15. For a description of the exhibition, see *Posters by Cassandre* (New York: The Museum of Modern Art, 1936).
16. Green, *Léger and the Avant-Garde*, p. 172.
17. For a reproduction, see Christian Zervos, *Pablo Picasso: Oeuvres de 1912 à 1917*, Vol. 2 (Paris, 1942), p. 208, pl. 444.
18. See Green, *Léger and the Avant-Garde*, p. 138, for a color reproduction.
19. *Ibid.*, pp. 208–209.
20. William S. Rubin, *The Paintings of Gerald Murphy* (New York: The Museum of Modern Art, 1974), p. 22.
21. For a color reproduction, see William S. Rubin, *Dada, Surrealism, and Their Heritage* (New York: The Museum of Modern Art, 1968), p. 34.
22. Green, *Léger and the Avant-Garde*, p. 205.
23. *Ibid.*, pp. 207–208.
24. A. M. Cassandre, ed., *Publicité Presenté par A. M. Cassandre*, Series: L'Art International d'Aujourd'hui, 12 (Paris: Charles Moreau, 1929).
25. For a color reproduction of the poster with the additional border, see Constantine and Fern, *Word and Image*, p. 83.

SELECTED BIBLIOGRAPHY

Boll, André. "A. M. Cassandre." *Médecine de France*, 198 (January 1969), pp. 25–37.

Cassandre, A. M. "A. M. Cassandre Describes His New 'Bifur' Type." *Commercial Art and Industry*, 8, no. 43 (January 1930), pp. 31–32.

———. "L'Affiche." *Les Cahiers Jaunes: Publication d'Art et de Littérature*, no. 3 (1933), pp. 15–21.

———. "L'Age de L'Affiche." *L'Affiche Illustré* (Collection Comoedia-Charpentier). Paris: Les Publications Techniques. 1944, p. 1.

———. *A. M. Cassandre: Peintre d'Affiches*. Introduction by Maximilien Vox. St. Gallen: Zollikofer & Cie, 1948.

———. "Art and Poster Art by A. M. Cassandre." *Gebrauchsgraphik*, 10, no. 1 (January 1933), pp. 4–5.

———. "Bifur Caractère de Publicité Dessiné par A. M. Cassandre." *Arts et Métiers Graphiques*, no. 9 (January 1929), p. 578.

———, ed. *Publicité Presenté par A. M. Cassandre* (Series: L'Art International d'Aujourd'hui, 12). Paris: Charles Moreau, 1929.

A. M. Cassandre. Amsterdam: Rijksakademie van Beeldende Kunsten, 1967.

Champigneulle, Bernard. "A. M. Cassandre." *Graphis*, 7, no. 34 (January 1951), pp. 12–23, 93–94.

Cheronnet, Louis. "Les Maîtres de l'Affiche: A. M. Cassandre." *L'Art Vivant* (November 15, 1926), pp. 854–855.

Constantine, Mildred, and Fern, Alan M. *Word and Image: Posters from the Collection of The Museum of Modern Art*. New York: The Museum of Modern Art, 1968.

Douglass, James C. "A. M. Cassandre: Golden Age of the Advertising Poster." *Print*, 23, no. 1 (January–February 1969), pp. 50–54.

Dupuy, R. L. "Les Affichists Français Contemporains: A. M. Cassandre." *Gebrauchsgraphik*, 4, no. 6 (June 1927), p. 47.

Exposition A. M. Cassandre. Paris: Musée des Arts Décoratifs, 1950.

"Exposition Loupot-Cassandre (Une)." *Arts et Métiers Graphiques*, no. 24 (July 15, 1931), pp. 309–319.

Französische Spielkarten des XX Jahrhunderts. Bielefeld: Deutsches Spielkarten Museum, 1955, pp. 13–19.

Gallo, Max. *The Poster in History*. New York: American Heritage Publishing Co., 1974.

Gerstner, Karl, and Kutter, Markus. *The New Graphic Art*. Vienna: Verlag Willy Verkauf, 1959.

Golding, John, and Green, Christopher. *Léger and Purist Paris*. London: Tate Gallery, 1970.

Green, Christopher. *Léger and the Avant-Garde*. New Haven and London: Yale University Press, 1976.

Henrion, F. H. K. "A Little Scandal in the Street." *The Penrose Annual*, no. 63 (1970), pp. 25–39.

Hillier, Bevis. *Posters*. New York: Stein & Day, 1969.

Hutchison, Harold F. *The Poster: an Illustrated History from 1860*. New York: The Viking Press, 1968.

Metzl, Ervine. *The Poster: Its History and Its Art*. New York: Watson-Guptill Publications, 1962.

Mouron, Henri. "A. M. Cassandre." *Le Club Français de la Medaillé*, Bulletin no. 41 (1973), pp. 100–107.

Müller-Brockmann, Josef. *A History of Visual Communication*. Teufen, Switzerland: Verlag Arthur Niggli, 1971.

———, and Shizuko. *History of the Poster*. Zürich: ABC Verlag, 1971.

Peignot, Charles. "Cassandre et la Typographie." *Médecine de France*, 198 (January 1969), pp. 38–40.

Posters by Cassandre. New York: The Museum of Modern Art, 1936.

"Projects for Four Posters: a Portfolio by A. M. Cassandre." *Fortune*, 15, no. 3 (March 1937), pp. 120–125.

Rickards, Maurice. *Posters of the Nineteen-Twenties*. New York: Walker & Co., 1968.

———. *The Rise and Fall of the Poster*. New York: McGraw-Hill Book Co., 1971.

Rosenblum, Robert. *Cubism and Twentieth-Century Art*. New York: Harry N. Abrams, 1961.

Schindler, Herbert. *Monografie des Plakats*. Munich: Süddeutscher Verlag, 1972.

Sembach, Klaus-Jürgen. *Style 1930: Elegance and Sophistication in Architecture, Design, Fashion, Graphics, and Photography*. New York: Universe Books, 1971.

Setlin, Percy. "American Posters and A. M. Cassandre." *PM*, 3, no. 5 (January 1937), pp. 17–22.

Snyder, Jerome. "Hall of Fame." In *51st Annual of Advertising, Editorial, and Television Arts and Design and the Inception of the Hall of Fame*. New York: Watson-Guptill, 1971, unpaged.

Valotaire, Marcel. "The Posters of A. M. Cassandre." *Commercial Art and Industry*, 4, no. 19 (January 1928), pp. 20–24.

Vox, Maximilien. "Influences de Bifur." *Arts et Métiers Graphiques*, no. 19 (September 15, 1930), pp. 32–36.

Zahar, Marcel. "L'Affiche de 1900 à 1939: Paul Colin, A. M. Cassandre." *Arts de France*, no. 17–18 (1947), pp. 30–46.

The Poster Art of A. M. CASSANDRE

All posters are lithographs with the exception of no. 34 (*Wagon-Bar*) and no. 49 (*Pernod Fils*), which are photo-offset combined with lithography.

1. *Sadac*. 1922. Hachard et Cie, Paris. 31½″ x 23⅝″ (80 x 60 cm). Collection Barry Friedman, Ltd., New York.

2. *Au Bûcheron: le Grand Magasin du Meuble.* 1923. Hachard et Cie, Paris. 59″ x 157½″ (150 x 400 cm). Collection Musée des Arts Décoratifs, Paris.

3. *PiVolo*. 1924. Hachard et Cie, Paris. 78¾" x 51³⁄₁₆" (200 x 130 cm). Collection Musée des Arts Décoratifs, Paris.

4. *Réglisse Florent*. 1925. Hachard et Cie, Paris. 60" x 37½" (152 x 95 cm). Collection Susan J. Pack.

5. *L'Intransigeant*. 1925. Hachard et Cie, Paris. 47¼" x 63" (120 x 160 cm). Collection Susan J. Pack.

6. *Golden Club*. c. 1925. Hachard et Cie, Paris. 78¾" x 51³⁄₁₆" (200 x 130 cm). Collection Susan J. Pack.

7. *Grand Sport: la Casquette Adoptée par Tous les Champions.* c. 1925. Hachard et Cie, Paris. 59″ x 46″ (150 x 116.8 cm). Collection Susan J. Pack.

8. *Société Anonyme de Gérance et d'Armement.* 1927. Hachard et Cie, Paris. 47¼″ x 31½″ (120 x 80 cm). Collection Reinhold-Brown Gallery, New York.

9. *Nord Express.* 1927. Hachard et Cie, Paris. 41⅜" x 29½" (105 x 75 cm). Collection Susan J. Pack.

10. *Étoile du Nord*. 1927. Hachard et Cie, Paris. 41⅜" x 29½" (105 x 75 cm). Collection Susan J. Pack.

11. *Nederlandsche Nyverheidsten Tentoonstelling (Nenyto)*. 1928. Nijgh en Van Ditmar. Rotterdam. 41⅜" x 29½" (105 x 75 cm). Collection Stedelijk Museum, Amsterdam.

12. *Statendam*. 1928. Nijgh en Van Ditmar, Rotterdam. 41⅜" x 29½" (105 x 75 cm). Collection Reinhold-Brown Gallery, New York.

13. *LMS Bestway*. 1928. McCorquodale & Co., Ltd., London. 39⅜" x 48¹³⁄₁₆" (100 x 124 cm). Collection Reinhold-Brown Gallery, New York.

14. *Écosse (par les trains deluxe LMS)*. 1928. Bemrose & Sons, Co., Ltd., Derby. 39¾" x 29¾" (101 x 75.5 cm). Collection Reinhold-Brown Gallery, New York.

15. *LMS The Best Way* (or *LMS Grande Bretagne*). 1928. L. Danel, Lille. 39⅜" x 24⁷⁄₁₆" (100 x 62 cm). Collection Reinhold-Brown Gallery, New York.

16. *Goedkoope Biljetten naar Londen*. 1928. Nijgh en Van Ditmar (?), Rotterdam. 39⅜″ x 24⁷⁄₁₆″ (100 x 62 cm). Collection Stedelijk Museum, Amsterdam.

17. *Sools: Maitre Chapelier*. 1929. Cie Artistique de Publicité, Paris. 94½" x 63" (240 x 160 cm). Photographed from the original gouache. Collection Barry Friedman, Ltd., New York. In the published version the face is brown, brick, and pink and the hat is green.

18. *Chemin de Fer du Nord*. 1929. L. Danel, Lille. 39⅜" x 24⁷⁄₁₆" & 78¾" x 51³⁄₁₆" (100 x 62 & 200 x 130 cm). Collection Reinhold-Brown Gallery, New York.

19. *La Route Bleue*. 1929. L. Danel, Lille. 39⅜" x 24⁷⁄₁₆" (100 x 62 cm). Collection Susan J. Pack.

20. *L'Oiseau Bleu.* 1929. L. Danel, Lille. 39⅜" x 24⁷⁄₁₆" (100 x 62 cm). Collection Reinhold-Brown Gallery, New York.

21. *R.A.I. Automobiel- & Motorrijwiel Tentoonstelling.* Designed 1929. Nijgh en Van Ditmar, Rotterdam. 47¼" x 31½" (120 x 80 cm). Collection Herbert Goldman.

22. *Champions du Monde.* 1930. B. Grasset, Paris. 25⁹⁄₁₆" x 19⁵⁄₁₆" (65 x 49 cm). Collection Kunstgewerbemuseum, Zürich.

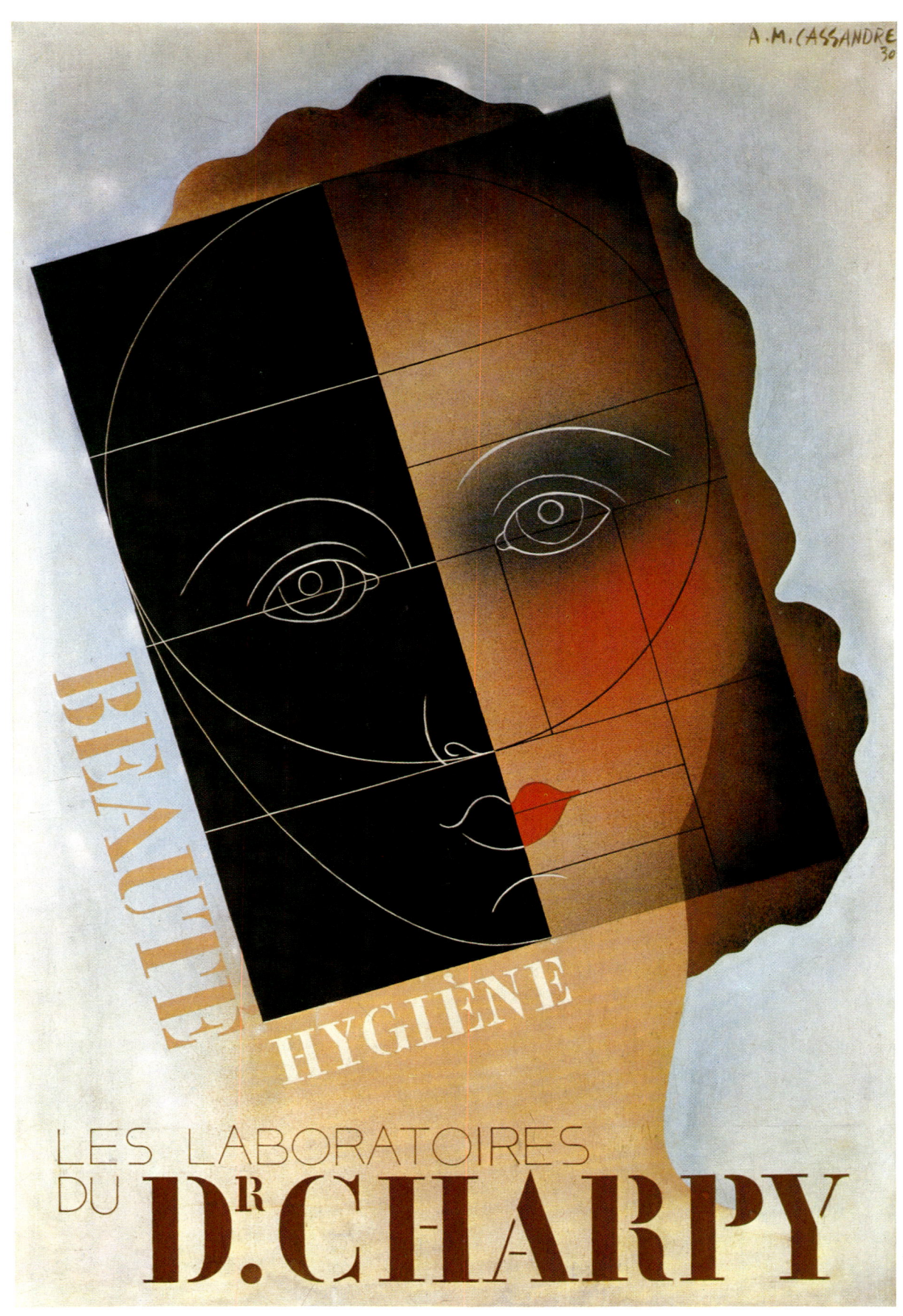

23. *Dr. Charpy*. 1930. Cie Artistique de Publicité, Paris. 94½" x 63" (240 x 160 cm). Photographed from the original gouache. Collection Richard F. Feiner. In the published version the style, position, and the text of the lettering were altered.

24. *Lys Chantilly*. 1930. L. Danel, Lille. 39⅜" x 24⁷⁄₁₆" (100 x 62 cm). Collection Kunstgewerbemuseum, Zürich.

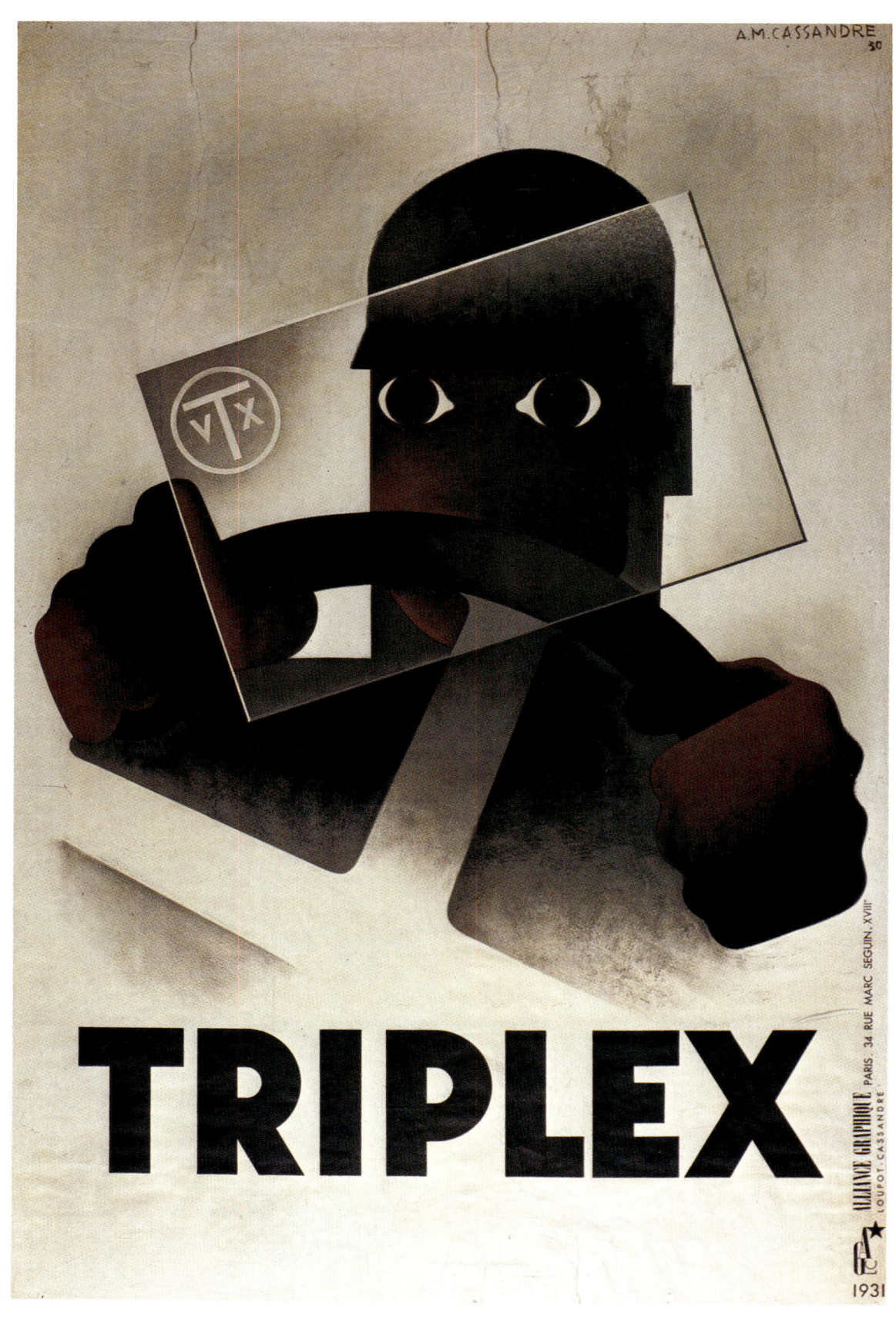

25. *Triplex*. Designed 1930. Alliance Graphique, Paris. 63″ x 47¼″ (160 x 120 cm). Collection Reinhold-Brown Gallery, New York.

26. *Flèche d'Argent: Aéropostale.* 1930. Société Anonyme Courbet, Paris. 39⅜" x 24⁷⁄₁₆" (100 x 62 cm). Collection Stedelijk Museum, Amsterdam.

27. *En Wagons-Lits.* 1930. L. Danel, Lille. 39⅜" x 24⁷⁄₁₆" (100 x 62 cm). Collection Reinhold-Brown Gallery, New York.

28. *Heemaf*. 1930. Nijgh en Van Ditmar, Rotterdam. 11¹³⁄₁₆″ x 7⅞″ & 51³⁄₁₆″ x 35⁷⁄₁₆″ (30 x 20 & 130 x 90 cm). Photographed from the original gouache. Collection Stedelijk Museum, Amsterdam.

29. *Spidoléine*. 1931. Alliance Graphique, Paris. 63" x 47¼" (160 x 120 cm). Collection The Museum of Modern Art, New York.

30. *Thomson: La Main-d'Oeuvre Électro-Domestique*. 1931. Alliance Graphique, Paris. 10⅝" x 7 1/16" & 47¼" x 31½" (27 x 18 & 120 x 80 cm). Collection Susan J. Pack.

31. *L' Atlantique*. 1931. Alliance Graphique, Paris. 39⅜" x 24⁷⁄₁₆" (100 x 62 cm). Collection Susan J. Pack.

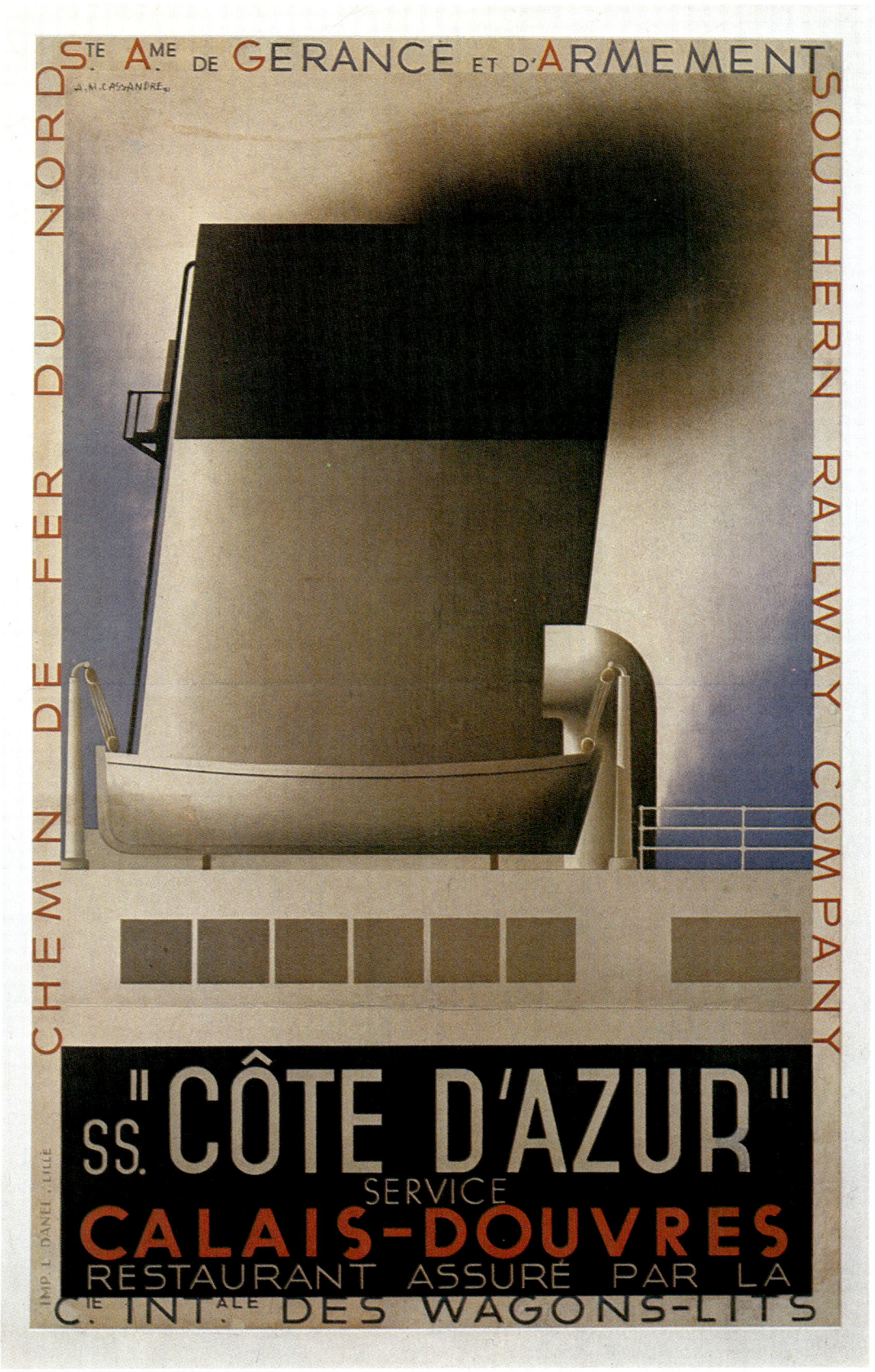

32. *S.S. Côte d'Azur.* 1931. Alliance Graphique, Paris. 39⅜" x 24⁷⁄₁₆" (100 x 62 cm). Collection Reinhold-Brown Gallery, New York.

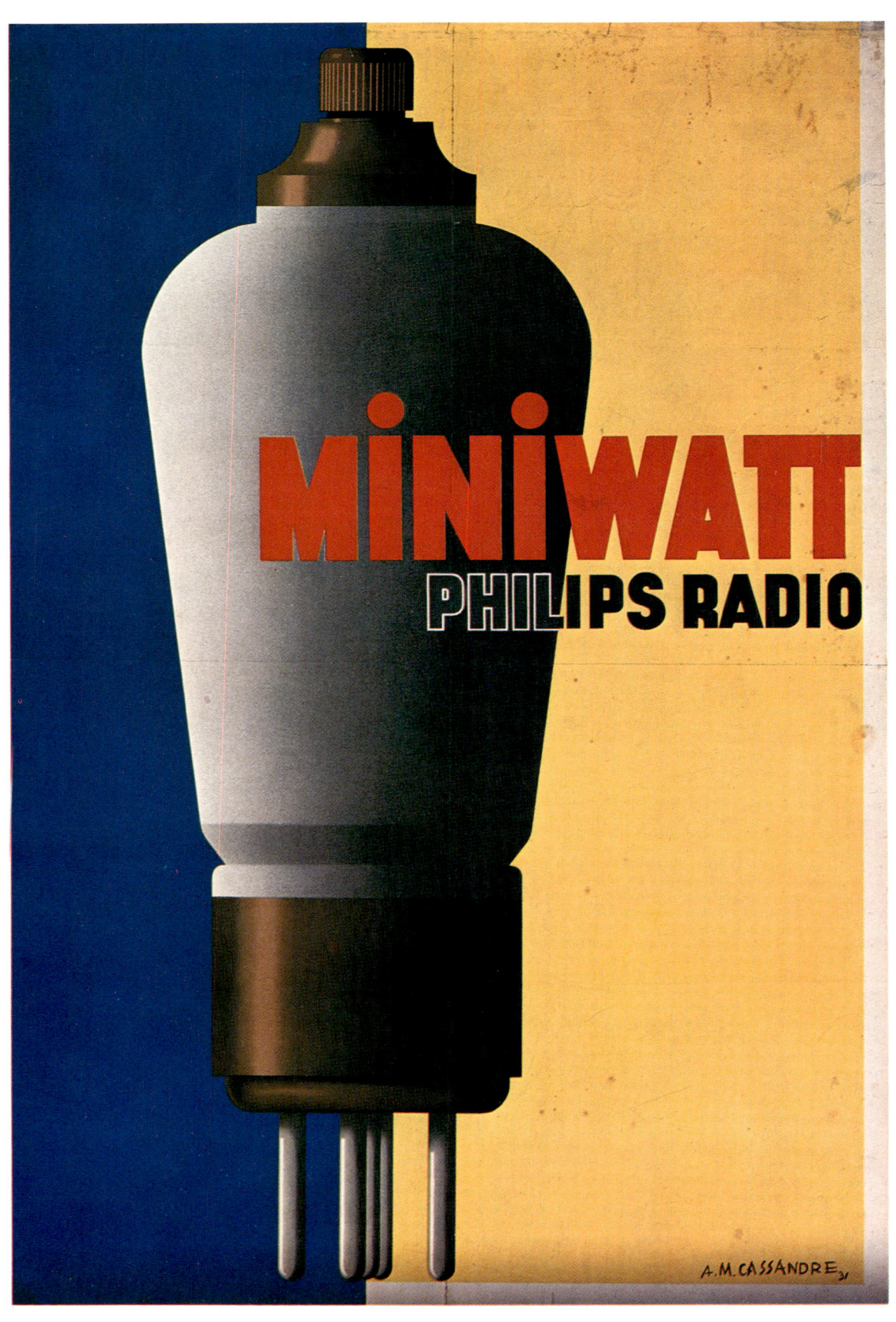

33. *Miniwatt: Philips Radio.* 1931. Alliance Graphique, Paris. 47¼″ x 31½″ (120 x 80 cm). Collection Kunstgewerbemuseum, Zürich.

34. *Wagon-Bar*. 1932. L. Danel, Lille. 39⅜" x 24⁷⁄₁₆" (100 x 62 cm). Photograph from original gouache and photomontage in the collection of Richard F. Feiner.

35. *Pathé: L'Enregistrement Électrique le Plus Perfectionné.* 1932. Alliance Graphique, Paris. 23⅝" x 15¾" & 94½" x 63" (60 x 40 & 240 x 160 cm). Collection Stedelijk Museum, Amsterdam.

36. *Air Orient.* 1932. Publisher not given. 23¾" x 20¾" (60.3 x 52.7 cm). Collection The Museum of Modern Art, New York.

37. *Dubo . . . Dubon . . . Dubonnet*. 1932. Alliance Graphique, Paris. Printed in several sizes. Collection The Museum of Modern Art, New York.

38. *Unic: Chaussures d'Hommes*. 1932. Alliance Graphique, Paris. 63″ x 47¼″ (160 x 120 cm). Collection Peter Rauch.

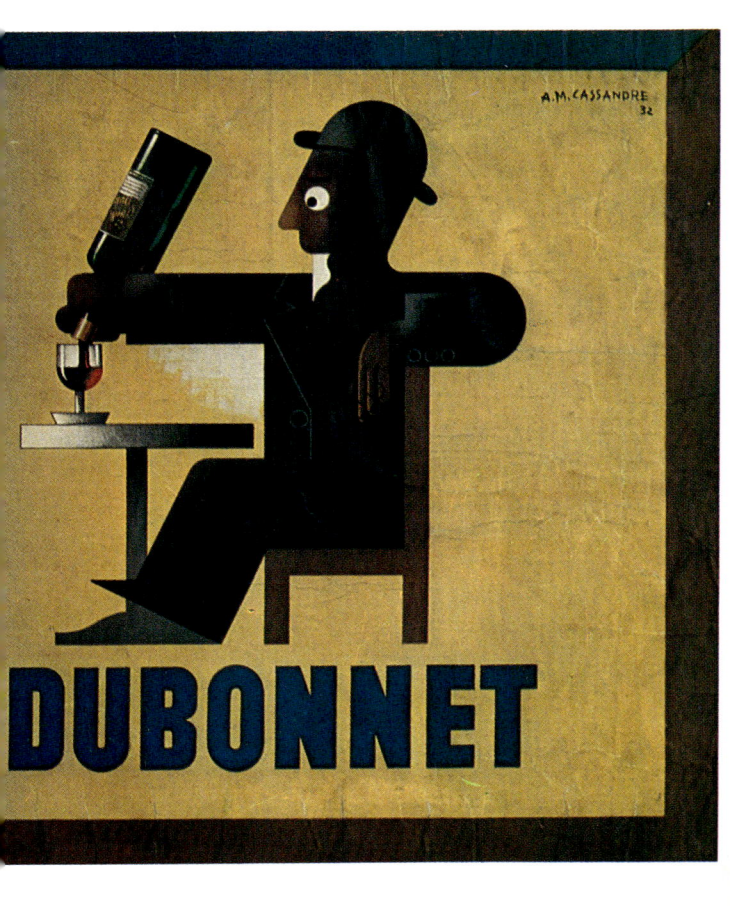

39. *Grande Quinzaine Internationale de Lawn-Tennis.* 1932. Alliance Graphique, Paris. 63″ x 47¼″ (160 x 120 cm). Collection Kunstgewerbemuseum, Zürich.

40. *Le Jour.* 1933. *Le Jour,* Paris. 47¼″ x 63″ (120 x 160 cm) and larger sizes. Collection Musée des Arts Décoratifs, Paris.

41. *Wagons Lits Cook*. 1933. Alliance Graphique, Paris. 39⅜″ x 24⁷⁄₁₆″ & 94½″ x 63″ (100 x 62 & 240 x 160 cm). Collection Reinhold-Brown Gallery, New York.

42. *Leroy*. 1933. Alliance Graphique, Paris. 59″ x 39⅜″ (150 x 100 cm). Collection Linda diLiberto.

43. *Angleterre.* 1934. Alliance Graphique, Paris. 126″ x 94½″ (320 x 240 cm). Collection Reinhold-Brown Gallery, New York.

44. *Price's Motorine*. 1934. Price's Motorine(?), London. 39⅜" x 24⁷⁄₁₆" (100 x 62 cm) and smaller. Collection Susan J. Pack.

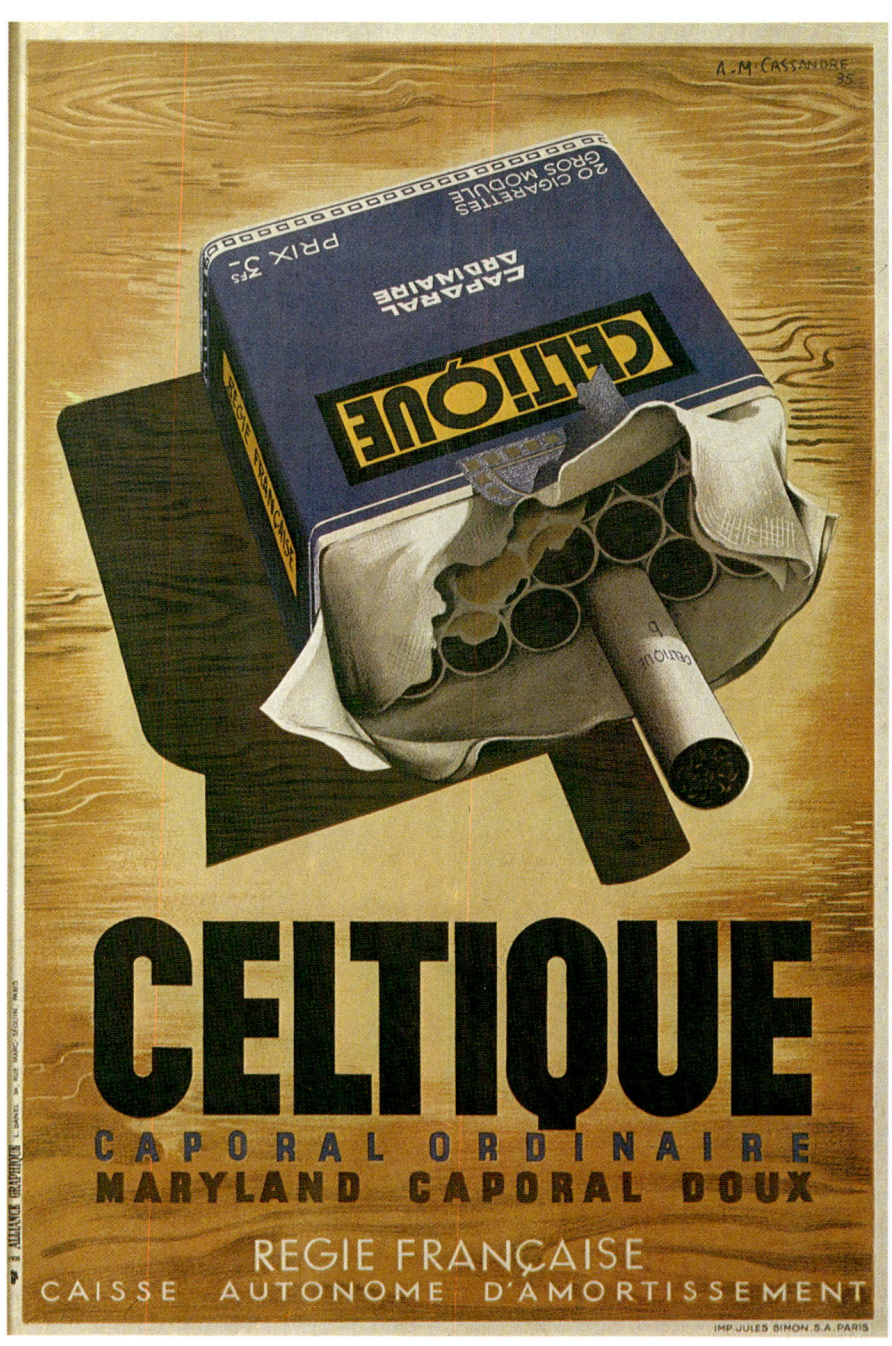

45. *Celtique Caporal Ordinaire.* Designed 1934. Alliance Graphique, Paris. 59" x 39⅜" (150 x 100 cm) and larger and smaller sizes. Collection Mr. and Mrs. David Bradford.

46. *Grandes Fêtes de Paris.* 1934. Alliance Graphique, Paris. 63" x 47¼" (160 x 120 cm). Collection David Bergman and Robert Helsley.

47. *Maison Prunier*. 1934. Alliance Graphique, Paris. 78¾″ x 48³⁄₁₆″ (200 x 124 cm). Collection The Museum of Modern Art, New York.

48. *À L'Eau avec un Peu de Cassis ou un Zeste de Citron* (Dubonnet). 1934. Alliance Graphique, Paris. 94½″ x 126″ (240 x 320 cm). Photograph taken from the original gouache. Collection Barry Friedman, Ltd., New York.

49. *Pernod Fils*. 1934. Alliance Graphique, Paris. 63" x 47¼" (160 x 120 cm). Collection Reinhold-Brown Gallery, New York.

50. *Sweepstake: Prix de l'Arc de Triomphe*. 1935. Alliance Graphique, Paris. 126″ x 94½″ (320 x 240 cm) and smaller. Collection Reinhold-Brown Gallery, New York.

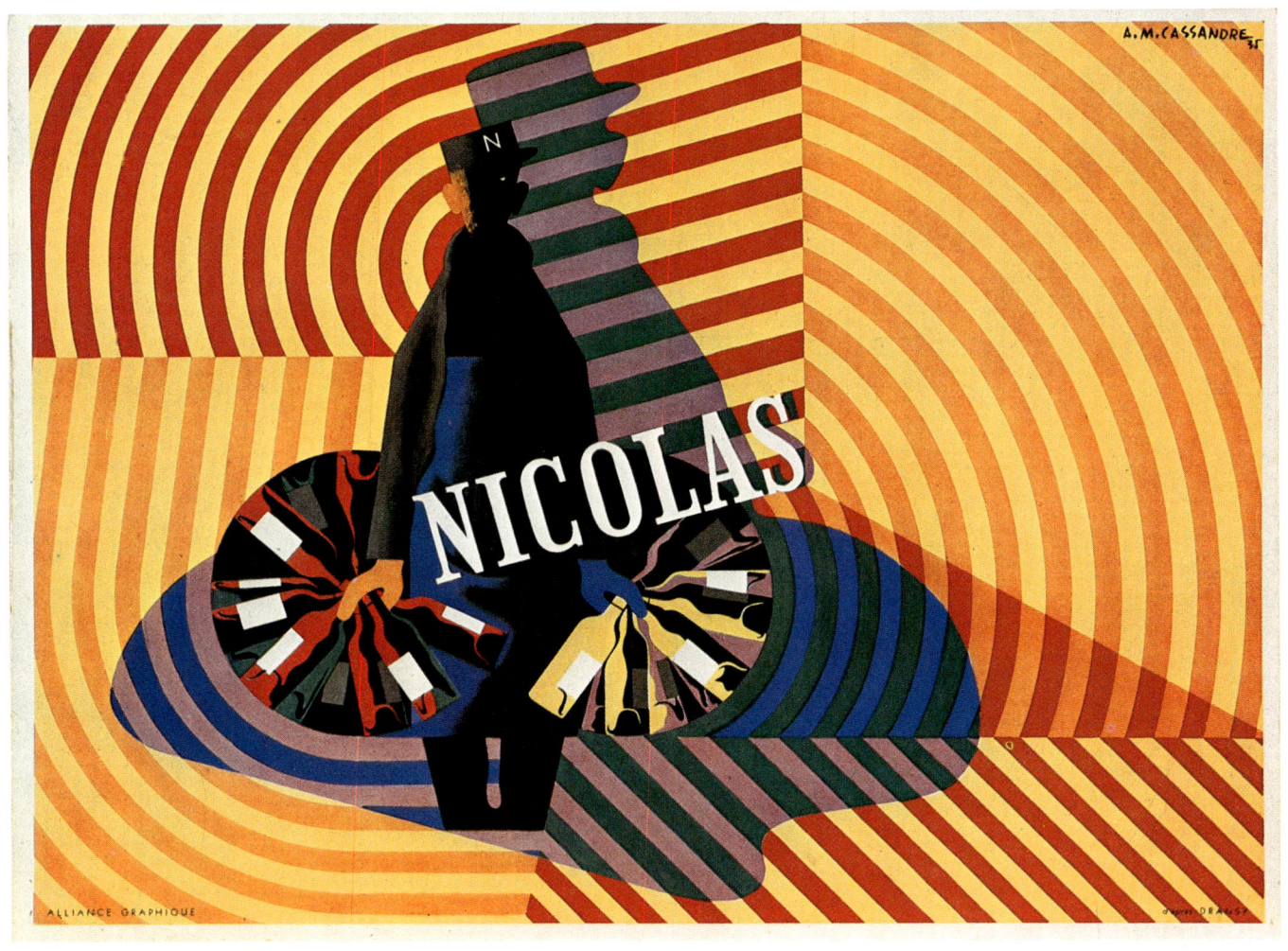

51. *Nicolas.* 1935. Alliance Graphique, Paris. 94½″ x 126″ (240 x 320 cm). Photograph taken from A. M. Cassandre and Blaise Cendrars, *La Spectacle est dans la Rue* (Paris: Draeger Frères, 1935).

52. *Fêtes de Paris.* 1935. Alliance Graphique, Paris. 63″ x 47¼″ (160 x 120 cm). and smaller. Collection David Bergman and Robert Helsley.

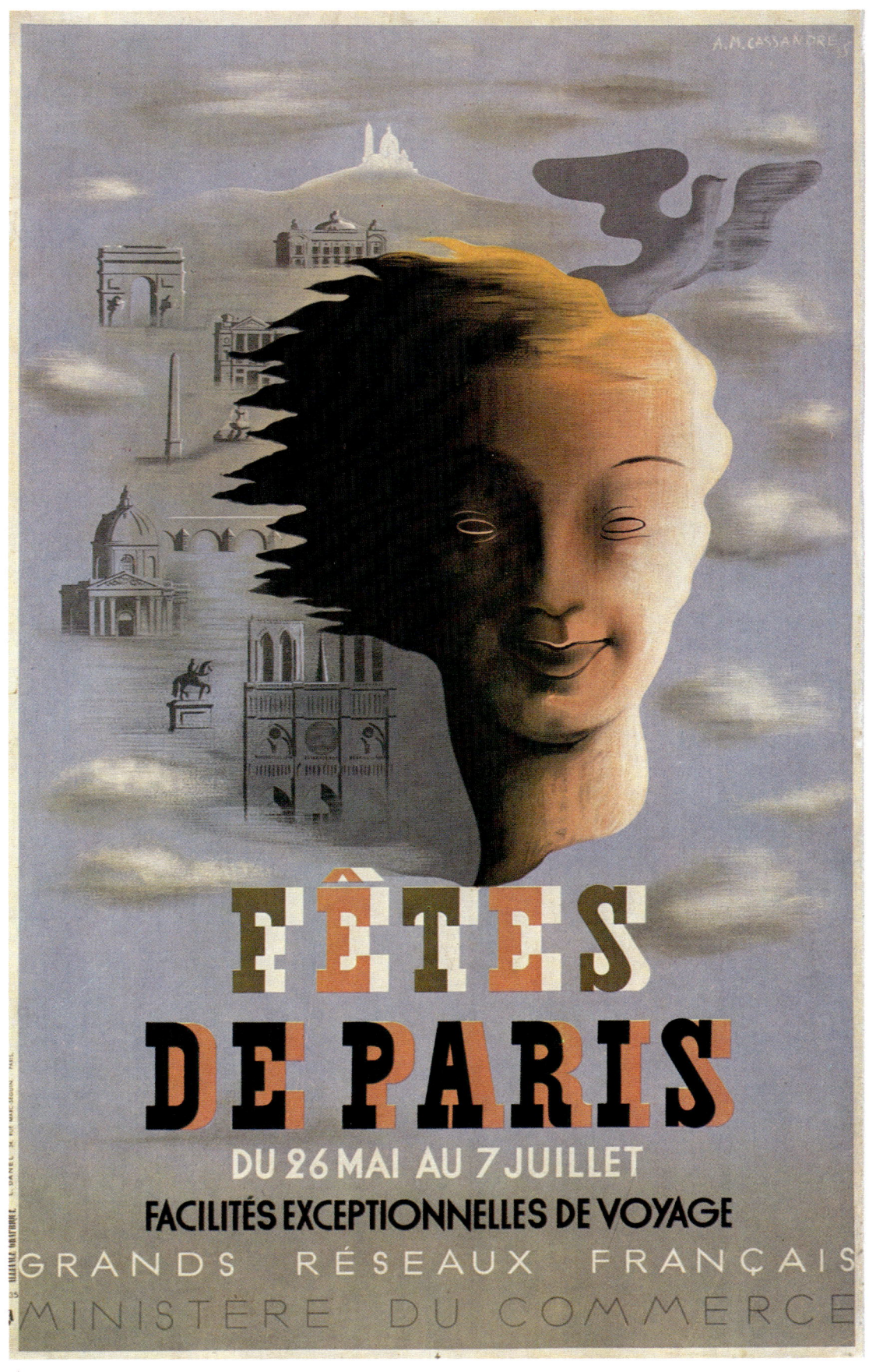

53. *Normandie*. 1935. Alliance Graphique, Paris. 39⅜″ x 24 7/16″ (100 x 62 cm). Collection Susan J. Pack.

54. *Paris*. 1935. Draeger Frères, Paris. 39⅜″ x 24 7/16″ (100 x 62 cm). Collection Reinhold-Brown Gallery, New York.

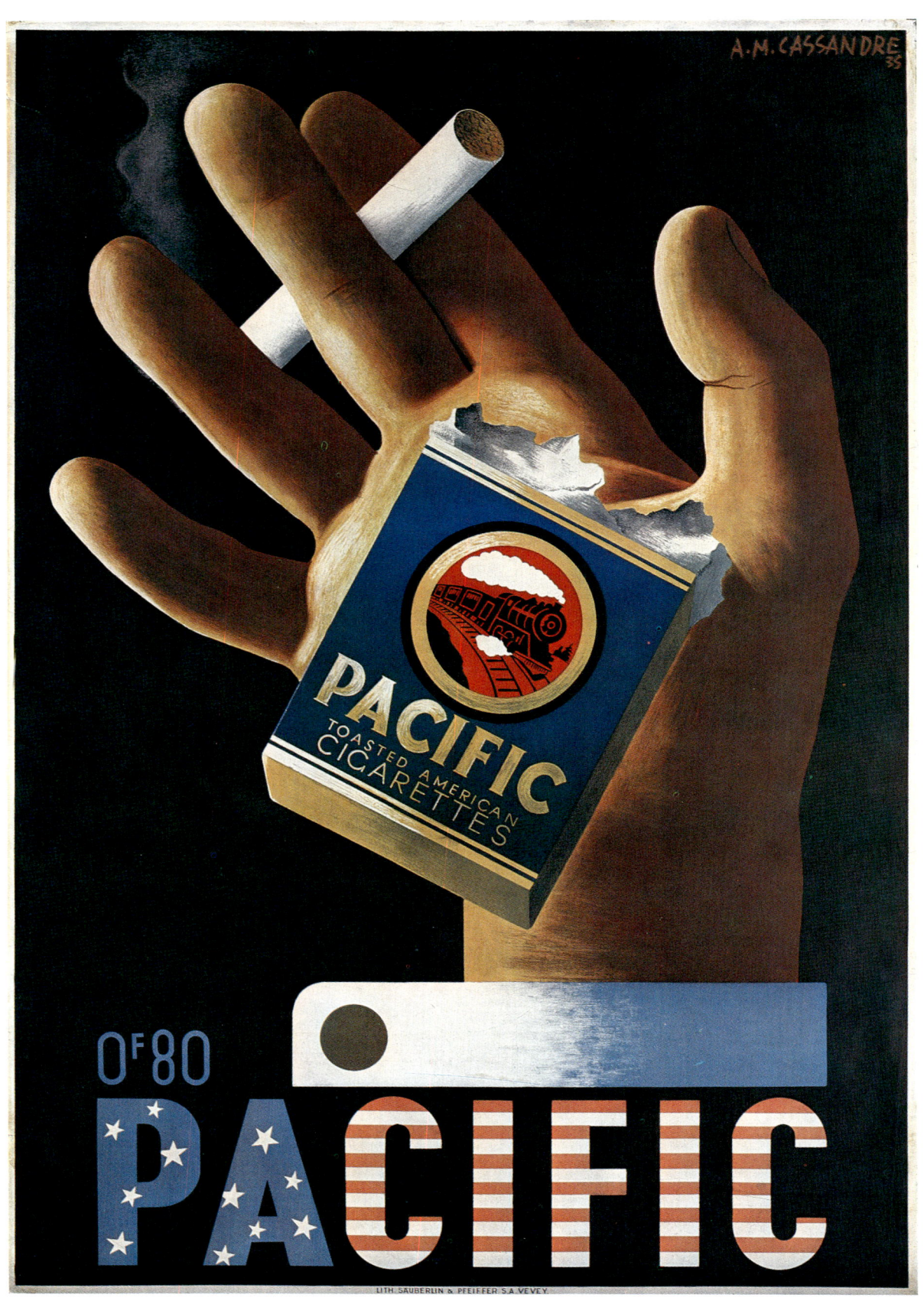

55. *Pacific Cigarettes*. 1935. Säuberlin & Pfeiffer, S.A., Vevey. 50½″ x 35⁷⁄₁₆″ (128 x 90 cm). Collection Kunstgewerbemuseum, Zürich.

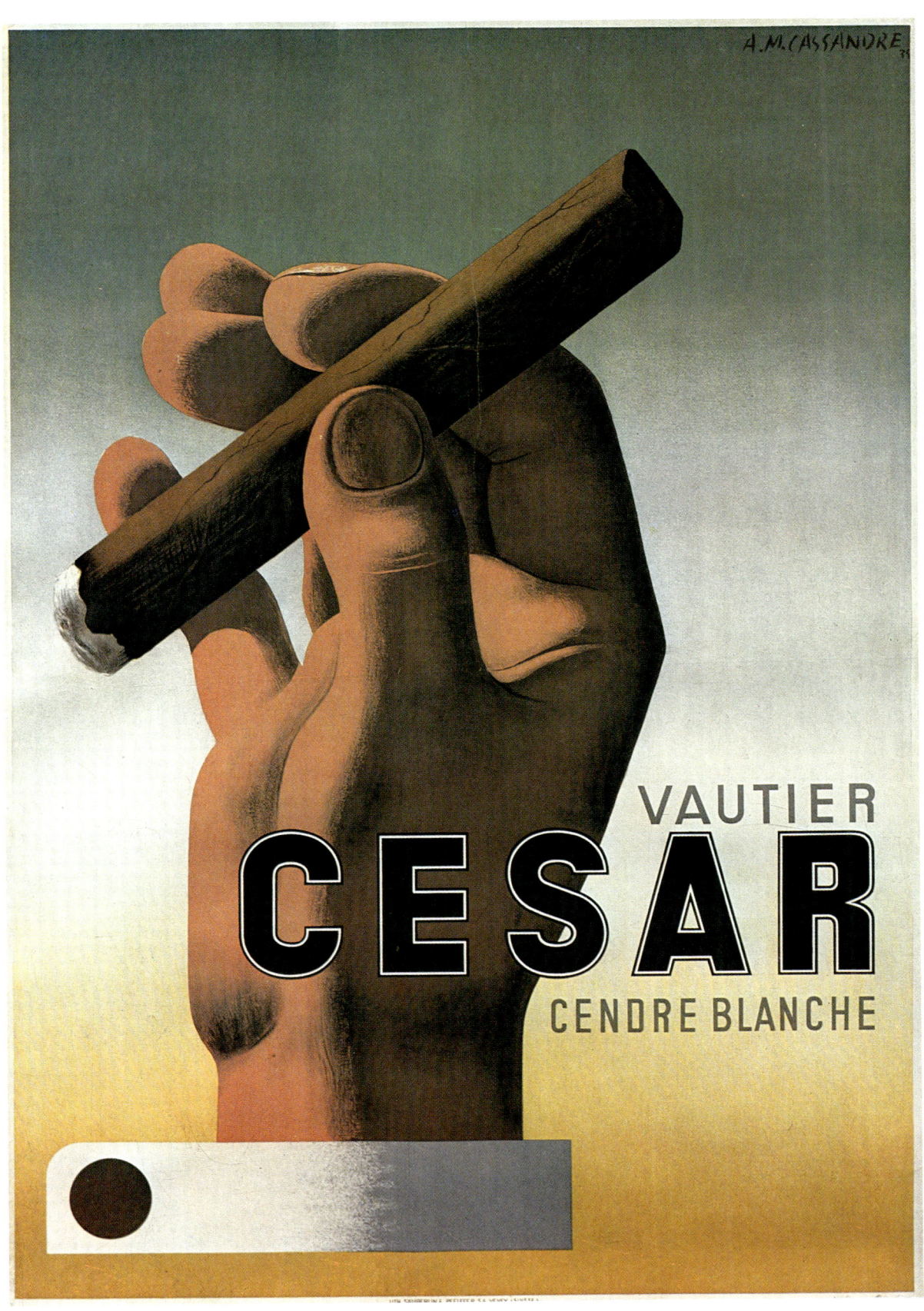

56. *Vautier César.* 1935. Vautier Frères, S.A., Yverdon. 50½" x 357/16" (128 x 90 cm). Collection Susan J. Pack.

57. *Kina Nectar*. 1936. Draeger Frères, Paris. 47¼″ x 63″ (120 x 160 cm). Collection Frank Latorre.

58. *Italia*. 1936. Officina Grafiche Coen & Cia, Milan. 39⅜″ x 24⁷⁄₁₆″ (100 x 62 cm). Collection Stephan Ganeles, New York.

59. *Italia*. 1936. Officina Grafiche Coen & Cia, Milan. 39⅜" x 24⁷⁄₁₆" (100 x 62 cm). Collection Stephan Ganeles, New York.

60. *Italia-Cosulich*. 1936. Officina Grafiche Coen & Cia, Milan. 39⅜" x 24⁷⁄₁₆" (100 x 62 cm). Collection Barry Friedman, Ltd., New York.

INDEX TO THE COLOR PLATES

Air Orient, 63
À L'Eau avec un Peu de Cassis ou un Zeste de Citron, 75
Angleterre, 70
Atlantique, L', 58
Au Bûcheron, 28–29
Celtique Caporal Ordinaire, 72
Champions du Monde, 49
Chemin de Fer du Nord, 45
Dr. Charpy, 50
Dubo . . . Dubon . . . Dubonnet, 64–65
Écosse (par les trains deluxe LMS), 41
En Wagons-Lits, 54
Étoile du Nord, 37
Fêtes de Paris, 79
Flèche d'Argent: Aéropostale, 53
Goedkoope Biljetten naar Londen, 43
Golden Club, 33
Grande Quinzaine Internationale de Lawn-Tennis, 66
Grandes Fêtes de Paris, 73
Grand Sport, 34
Heemaf, 55
Intransigeant, L', 32
Italia, 85
Italia (another version), 86
Italia-Cosulich, 87
Jour, Le, 67
Kina Nectar, 84
Leroy, 69
LMS Bestway, 40
LMS The Best Way (LMS Grande Bretagne), 42

Lys Chantilly, 51
Maison Prunier, 74
Miniwatt: Philips Radio, 60
Nederlandsche Nyverheidsten Tentoonstelling (Nenyto), 38
Nicolas, 78
Nord Express, 36
Normandie, 80
Oiseau Bleu, L', 47
Pacific Cigarettes, 82
Paris, 81
Pathé: L'Enregistrement Électrique le Plus Perfectionné, 62
Pernod Fils, 76
PiVolo, 30
Price's Motorine, 71
R.A.I. Automobiel- & Motorrijwiel Tentoonstelling, 48
Réglisse Florent, 31
Route Bleue, La, 46
Sadac, 27
Société Anonyme de Gérance et d'Armement, 35
Sools: Maître Chapelier, 44
Spidoléine, 56
S.S. Côte d'Azur, 59
Statendam, 39
Sweepstake: Prix de l'Arc de Triomphe, 77
Thomson: La Main-d'Oeuvre Électro-Domestique, 57
Triplex, 52
Unic: Chaussures d'Hommes, 65
Vautier César, 83
Wagon-Bar, 61
Wagons Lits Cook, 68

ROBERT BROWN is co-owner, with Susan Reinhold, of the Reinhold-Brown Gallery in New York, which specializes in fine and rare poster art from the turn of the century through the 1930s. He compiled the bibliography for The Minneapolis Institute of Arts' "Art Deco" show (1971) and wrote the introduction to *Art Deco International* (1978).

SUSAN REINHOLD is co-owner of the Reinhold-Brown Gallery in New York. Among the exhibitions she has mounted are "Posters of the Vienna Secession" (1975), "The Posters of Ludwig Hohlwein" (1976), "Architecture and the Poster" (1977), and "The Posters of A. M. Cassandre" (1978).